*The Author wishes to acknowledge the advice
and help given by
Mr. Roy Lancaster of Hillier & Sons,
Winchester, and Mr. H. J. Welch, author of
'Dwarf Conifers—A Complete Handbook'
(Faber and Faber)
and owner of the Pygmy Pinetum,
Devizes, Wiltshire.*

*The Publishers wish to thank
Michael Warren for his
outstanding photography undertaken
specially for this book
and would also like to express
their appreciation in being allowed
to take photographs
at the following gardens,*

*ENGLAND
Bressingham Gardens, Diss, Norfolk
(Mr. Alan Bloom)*

*Mr. R. S. Corley
Coombe Cottage, Naphill, High Wycombe
Buckinghamshire*

*'Foxhollow', Westwood Road, Windlesham
Surrey
(Mr. John F. Letts)*

*Garden House Farm, Drinkstone,
Nr. Bury St. Edmunds, Suffolk
(Mr. F. G. Barcock)*

*Mr. R. Hawkins, Bridge Farm, Brent Eleigh
Lavenham, Suffolk*

*Jermyns Garden and Arboretum, Jermyns Lane
Ampfield, Nr. Romsey, Hampshire
(Hillier & Sons Ltd.)*

*The Pygmy Pinetum, Devizes, Wiltshire
(Mr. H. J. Welch)*

*The Royal Horticultural Society Gardens
Ripley, Wisley, Surrey
(The Director)*

*Talbot Manor, Fincham, King's Lynn, Norfolk
(Mr. Maurice Mason)*

*U.S.A.
Longwood Gardens, Kennet Square, Pennsylvania
(The Director)*

*FRANCE
Pépinières Croux, Val d'Aulnay
Chatenay-Malabry*

Pépinières St. Antoine, Ervy-le-Chatel

COVER PHOTOGRAPH:
Conifers in the Dell Garden
at Bressingham, Norfolk, England

INSIDE FRONT COVER:
A view of large growing conifers in the
garden of Pépinières St. Antoine
at Ervy-le-Chatel, France.

INSIDE BACK COVER:
A view of dwarf conifers and heathers
in the Author's garden
at Bressingham.

CONIFERS FOR YOUR GARDEN

by Adrian Bloom

FLORAPRINT Ltd, CALVERTON, NOTTINGHAM

Adrian Bloom
is one of the few men in
horticulture who can be seen to
have vision and foresight. His collection
of dwarf conifers, built up
over the past ten years,
his artistic garden use of them
and his skill in commercial production
of top quality specimens in
great numbers, are matched by few others,
save perhaps his father who has done for
herbaceous plants what Adrian is
now doing for conifers.
The very rapid
development of the conifer
interest at Bressingham, near Diss
in Norfolk, including the heather and
conifer garden appendage to the
famous 'Dell Garden' against the previous
herbaceous plant domination, gives
proof to the faith he has in
conifers and the important part he feels they
have to play in modern plantings.
Having worked in both
European countries and the
United States, his personal experience and
knowledge of both plants and people is
considerable. This, coupled with
his friendly and open personality has
enabled practical experience,
the best sources of information on
correct nomenclature, and good advice
to be brought together in a way
that only he could do.
Adrian Bloom's enthusiasm
for these plants is contagious and
his written words, plus the
coloured illustrations, many of
which were photographed in his garden,
are a shot in the arm for
addicts and experimenters
looking for excitement.

SBN : 903001 01 2

What are Conifers?

What are Conifers?
The name "Conifer" comes from the
latin and means "cone bearing", so
although it is often thought that all
conifers are evergreen, some such as the
larch drop their leaves in autumn.
Among the conifers are some of the
smallest and certainly the biggest of
living woody plants.
Conifers will often live to a great age
and such is the variety of colour and
form available that they can provide a
valuable and fascinating addition to
any garden.

An example of the effective use of dwarf and slow growing conifers in the Pygmy Pinetum, Devizes, Wiltshire . . .

LARGE, SLOW GROWING AND DWARF CONIFERS

Because of the great range in size and rates of growth it is necessary to point out in this book the approximate growth of each conifer after 10 years and its ultimate height.

For this reason I have graded the conifers into 3 main groups:

1. LARGE, i.e. growing 3m. in 10 years, or ultimately over 12m.

2. MEDIUM, i.e. growing between 1·50–3m. in 10 years. It is more difficult to determine ultimate height here as some may eventually reach 12m. or more after 30 or more years.

3. DWARF, i.e. growing less than 1·50m. in 10 years. Among this range there are quite considerable variations.

Further to these 3 categories there are *PROSTRATE* and *SEMI-PROSTRATE* forms in which a 10 year growth span can also be estimated. These figures of course can only be approximations as soil, aspect, climate and rainfall are all contributing factors on growth.

SCALE

This breakdown into categories is necessary with conifers because it is important to know when choosing these plants what size they will attain. For instance it would be quite out of keeping, apart from being unwise, to plant *Sequoiadendron giganteum* in a small suburban garden. And yet this sort of thing is often done where an unwitting customer has picked a plant from a catalogue or garden centre without examining its credentials.

This book attempts to show what range of conifers is available to achieve the right effect for any given site. We have all seen an old yew (*Taxus*) a "Monkey Puzzle" (*Araucaria araucana*) or Christmas Tree (*Picea abies*) almost blotting out the light from the front windows of a house; one imagines that this was planted out of ignorance and not choice. Often enough the person who has planted the offending tree has since moved on!

It pays to plan ahead outside just as much as inside the house. With the wide range of plants available it is important to choose carefully.

. . . and also in the Author's garden at Bressingham.

HOW TO SELECT YOUR CONIFERS

With conifers as with all other plants it pays to buy from a reputable nursery or garden centre. Beware of conifers advertised at very low prices. These will often turn out to be poor quality which, if they grow, will prove to be varieties quite unsuitable for the average small garden of today.

The advantage of buying plants in a garden centre is that a personal selection can be made and the plants are usually grown in containers so will mostly transplant more easily than those dug from the open ground. On the other hand the choice may be more limited from a garden centre than from a specialist grower. From whatever source a plant should look healthy and preferably be well shaped and "furnished". This latter term means that it should have foliage to the base of the plant.

Many conifers, particularly cultivars of *Chamaecyparis lawsoniana*, once having lost foliage at the base will not regain it.

Most nurseries and garden centres include a range of conifers in their catalogue or on their premises, but it would be advisable, in fact necessary, to go to a specialist to obtain many of the species and cultivars shown in this book. To my knowledge all of the specimen plants shown in the colour pages are available in this country, although to find some of them may take a little searching through specialist catalogues. A few of the more unusual plants are included because I feel they are worthy of wider recognition, but it is far beyond the means and aims of this book to be a complete textbook on all the species and cultivars of conifers grown.

It is hoped rather to stimulate and interest the gardener in conifers as garden plants and show what can be achieved within this range.

NAMING OF CONIFERS

This is perhaps an appropriate place to mention what to some people is the greatest drawback to a full appreciation of conifers—their names!

All plants must of course have botanical names. Unfortunately the "Common" names that the average gardener prefers to use whenever possible are seldom available in the case of conifers (especially the cultivated forms), so the latin names must be used. These names consist of two, three or possibly more latin-form words, sometimes of generous length, and this fact and the confusion in some cases as to which is the *correct* name has not helped their popularity.

To the discerning gardener the correct name for a plant is all important and for him to receive *two* different plants under the same name or the same plant under different names from one or more sources is irritating to say the least. The difficulty has been that until recently even the nurserymen were almost as confused as the gardener!

However, in the last few years two books on the subject of conifers have been written which go a long way to stabilizing their nomenclature and I have attempted to follow the lines laid down in 'Dwarf Conifers' by H. J. Welch (published by Faber and Faber Ltd.) and 'Manual of Cultivated Conifers' by P. Den Ouden and Dr. B. K. Boom (published by Martinus Nijhoff, The Hague). Mr. Welch is particularly good on the subject and any reader wishing to look closely into dwarf conifers would do well to obtain his book.

Unfamiliarity with the names of conifers of course should not deter anyone from buying them, but it does help to have some idea of what names mean and why they can be lengthy and involved.

Conifers are classified by the botanists in the same way as all other plants, but here we need only concern ourselves with the ranks of genus and species.

Genera. This the plural of Genus, contains one or more and up to a great number of species grouped together and all having certain basic characteristics in common.

Examples of genera include the following—*Cedrus, Chamaecyparis, Picea* and *Thuja*.

Species. Plants in nature forming a closely knit group, freely interbreeding and separated from their nearest related groups are known as a species. Taking the genus *Chamaecyparis* as an example, this contains a total of six generally accepted species, *C. formosensis; C. lawsoniana; C. nootkatensis; C. obtusa; C. pisifera* and *C. thyoides*. All possess tiny green scale-like leaves borne in large flattened sprays and small cones composed of several shield-like scales.

Varieties. Some species are very variable in the wild, some of these variations being distinct enough to be regarded separately as varieties. A typical example is the Japanese "Hinoki Cypress"—*Chamaecyparis obtusa*. In the mountains of the island of Formosa grows a distinct variety of this species known as *C. obtusa* var. *formosana* differing mainly in its smaller leaves and cones.

Cultivars. The term cultivar is used to describe those plants which have arisen usually in cultivation as hybrids, sports or as chance seedlings. The term also includes plants which have been specially selected in the wild for their distinctive shape, form or colour and which are maintained in cultivation by vegetative means.

A cultivar name is normally included in single quotation marks when written, e.g. the names 'Ellwoodii', 'Pottenii' and 'Wisselii', which are all cultivars of *Chamaecyparis lawsoniana*.

According to the Cultivar Code laid down by the botanists, no conifer named after January 1st 1959, is allowed to be latinized. Conifers should have fancy or descriptive names such a *Juniperus scopulorum* 'Skyrocket' or *Chamaecyparis lawsoniana* 'Green Pillar'. Whilst to some these may sound somewhat undignified names to apply to conifers, it does make the plants more easily identifiable and often helps to increase their popularity.

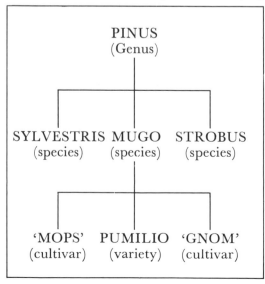

PINUS
(Genus)

SYLVESTRIS MUGO STROBUS
(species) (species) (species)

'MOPS' PUMILIO 'GNOM'
(cultivar) (variety) (cultivar)

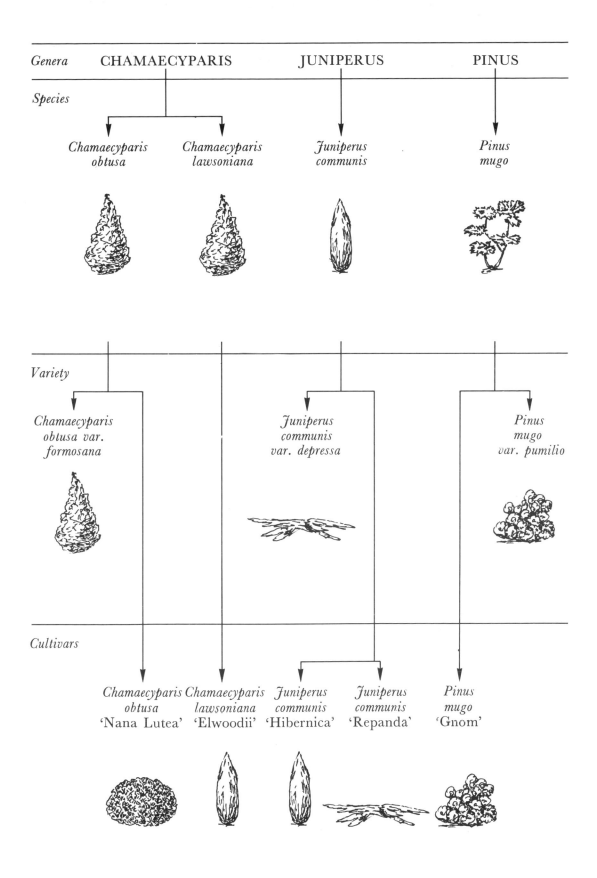

| *Genera* | CHAMAECYPARIS | | JUNIPERUS | PINUS |

Species

| *Chamaecyparis obtusa* | *Chamaecyparis lawsoniana* | *Juniperus communis* | *Pinus mugo* |

Variety

| *Chamaecyparis obtusa var. formosana* | *Juniperus communis var. depressa* | *Pinus mugo var. pumilio* |

Cultivars

| *Chamaecyparis obtusa* 'Nana Lutea' | *Chamaecyparis lawsoniana* 'Elwoodii' | *Juniperus communis* 'Hibernica' | *Juniperus communis* 'Repanda' | *Pinus mugo* 'Gnom' |

As so many dwarf and slow growing conifers are included in this book, and because in many ways they are suited to the modern garden, it is necessary perhaps to explain how some of these forms came about.

How is it for instance, that some conifers only grow 30cm. in 20 or 30 years, when others attain a height of 15m. in the same time?

To answer this as clearly and concisely as possible it is perhaps best to outline the various ways in which various forms occur.

Seedlings. Although it is not generally known conifers do flower and from these cones are produced. These of course vary from species to species as in other plants. Certain conifers are grown from seed, particularly for forestry purposes, such as the "Scots Pine", *Pinus sylvestris*.

In a single batch of seed from a *Chamaecyparis lawsoniana* cultivar however, individual plants might occur showing a considerable variation of shape, size or colour, and in this way many new cultivars have arisen. These variations however will not come true from seed and they therefore must be propagated by cuttings and sometimes grafting, to obtain more plants similar to the selected "clone". Cultivars of *Chamaecyparis lawsoniana* have come to us in this way, and also many other conifer species have produced cultivars from seed.

It has often happened that cultivars so similar as to be almost indistinguishable from each other have been introduced to the public, which is unfortunate as it has often lead to confusion.

Juvenile Fixations. This term sounds more as though it should belong in a book on psychology, but it is also applied to a certain type of conifer! Some seedling plants retain their "juvenile" foliage, that is the type of foliage that first breaks from the seed, which is quite unlike the adult foliage of the parent plant. *Chamaecyparis pisifera* 'Squarrosa Sulphurea' is and example of this type. This cultivar arose as a seedling from *Chamaecyparis pisifera*. These juvenile fixations will often revert to the adult form by throwing up a strong leading shoot To keep the dwarf or juvenile form this leading shoot should be cut away as soon as it becomes apparent.

Picea mariana 'Nana', normally one of the slowest growing of conifers throwing a "reverting" leading shoot. If not pruned or cut off at the base it will grow into the adult form of the plant shown below. This plant began its reversion four years previously and is now 1,5 m. high.

"Sports" and "Witches Brooms". Again terms more often associated elsewhere. A "sporting" branch is one which differs from normal. It may have leaves which are larger, smaller, differently arranged, or differently coloured than the typical branch. If this branch or shoot is carefully detached with a knife and rooted as a cutting, it will often produce a plant which might be introduced in time as a new cultivar. These new cultivars can also revert to the original form particularly those with yellow or variegated leaves which are often less vigorous than the parent plant.

Some genera, such as *Picea* and *Pinus* will throw "Witches Brooms"—congested growth on the branch of an older tree. If this can be detached and propagated successfully it may produce a cultivar worthy of introduction to the public.

Alpine or Mountain forms. Some comparatively dwarf conifers that exist where the climate is extremely harsh, such as in high alpine regions or in the tundra, retain their habit even when grown in gardens with more favourable situations. *Pinus mugo* var. *pumilo* (see page 110) is one of these and has proved one of the most useful dwarf conifers.

Cultivariants. Mr. H. J. Welch coined the phrase which aptly describes a further method which has produced "new" cultivars. If cuttings are taken, for instance, from a specimen of *Chamaecyparis lawsoniana* 'Ellwoodii', some at the base of the plant and some at the top, the resultant plants will in all probability have different habits. The tip cuttings will produce plants of taller and thinner growth, the basal cuttings will produce plants which are much slower and more compact. In many cases these habits will remain constant for some years, although generally the dwarfer plants will grow away in time to resemble the parent plant; it does mean however, that some named cultivars can and do vary considerably in habit.

Into the category of "cultivariants" may also be classed certain plants which would normally grow upright with a distinct leader, but because lateral shoots have been used for grafting, will often remain prostrate or semi-prostrate. Although sometimes a prostrate plant is not always intended to be such, when propagated such forms can be most attractive. To obtain a leader or main vertical shoot, grafted plants such as the *Picea pungens* cultivars, *Cedrus atlantica* 'Glauca', and some cultivars of *Abies* should be trained upwards until a leader is firmly established.

A large "Witches Broom" on a "Scots Pine", Pinus sylvestris.

An example of cultivariants in two specimens of Chamaecyparis Lawsoniana 'Ellwoodii' showing differing habits.

For the larger garden a small woodland area can be created. Space specimens carefully to allow for future growth.

The medium-sized conifers can be used to effect as a background to a garden in a natural setting in grass as shown in this photograph at Bressingham Gardens.

As a screen or a windbreak. This planting is mainly x Cupressocyparis leylandii which after eight years have Reached well over 6m.

Opposite page: Conifers used as a ground cover. The Juniperus horizontalis 'Glauca', growing prostrate between two semi-prostrate J. x media 'Pfitzeriana Aurea' disguises a manhole cover and at the same time adds an attractive focal point in the garden.

How to make the most of Conifers

This book is mainly concerned with garden conifers and therefore there is a larger concentration of medium, slow growing and dwarf conifers shown in the colour pages and described in the text.

For the larger garden there should be room for either *Cedrus deodara* or the "Blue Cedar" *Cedrus atlantica* 'Glauca'. There is no reason why there shouldn't be room for these for some years in the smaller garden also, but with both eventually reaching 20–30m. and a spread of roughly half that, the temptation is best resisted. Whilst it is easy to advise cutting the tree down after some years, when the size becomes embarrassing, it is not so easily achieved when the time comes. In some funny way one gets attached to a tree after having watched it grow for 30 years!

There is such a wide range of conifers that can be grown that it pays to choose carefully. The photographs shown alongside this text demonstrates uses to which conifers can be put. If there is an all purpose plant the conifer must be it; it has the decided advantage of being evergreen (apart from several notable exceptions) so one has colour and form the year round; it provides a background and maturity to any garden, and lastly but not least, most conifers increase in value as they get older.

It is not necessary to explain in detail what is evident from the photographs—the uses to which conifers can be put.

The advantage of planting dwarf and slow growing conifers has become very evident in recent years, primarily because they are

continued on p. 12

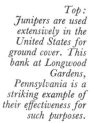

Top:
Junipers are used extensively in the United States for ground cover. This bank at Longwood Gardens, Pennsylvania is a striking example of their effectiveness for such purposes.

Middle:
The dwarf and slow growing conifers can add extra dimension and interest to the heather garden, giving an all-year-round display of form and colour. View of the author's garden four years after planting.

Bottom:
Dwarf conifers add permananence and interest in the rock garden. Many of the larger specimens in this photograph taken at the R.H.S. Gardens, Wisley, Surrey, are over 50 years old.

Opposite page.
Top:
Some conifers are well suited as "architectural" plants. This Juniperus scopulorum 'Skyrocket' makes an excellent focal point in a garden where it is surrounded by low growing plants.

Middle:
Thuja plicata used as a hedge to give both shelter to the heather garden and to divide this from the tennis court behind.

Bottom:
· A careful selection of conifers must be made for smaller rock gardens. This view of Mr. R. S. Corley's garden shows what can be achieved with only a small space available.

CONIFERS FOR SPECIAL PURPOSES

FOR WINDBREAKS
Chamaecyparis lawsoniana
x Cupressocyparis leylandii
Picea omorika
Pinus nigra
Thuja plicata

FOR HEDGES
Chamaecyparis lawsoniana
x Cupressocyparis leylandii
Taxus baccata
Tsuga canadensis
Tsuga heterophylla
Thuja plicata
Thuja occidentalis

FOR THE SMALLER ROCK GARDEN
Abies balsamea 'Hudsonia'
Chamaecyparis lawsoniana 'Minima Aurea'
Chamaecyparis obtusa 'Nana'
Chamaecyparis pisifera 'Nana'
Cryptomeria japonica 'Vilmoriniana'
Juniperus communis 'Compressa'
Picea glauca 'Albertiana Conica'
Picea abies 'Gregoryana'
Picea abies 'Nidiformis'
Picea mariana 'Nana'
Pinus sylvestris 'Beuvronensis'
Thuja plicata 'Rogersii'

FOR WINTER COLOUR
Cedrus atlantica 'Glauca'
Chamaecyparis lawsoniana 'Lanei'
Chamaecyparis lawsoniana 'Minima Aurea'
Chamaecyparis lawsoniana 'Pygmaea Argentea'
Picea pungens glauca—named cultivars
Taxus baccata 'Fastigiata Standishii'
Thuja occidentalis 'Lutea Nana'
Thuja occidentalis 'Lutescens'
Thuja occidentalis 'Rheingold'
Thuja plicata 'Stoneham Gold'

FOR GROUND COVER—prostrate
Juniperus communis 'Repanda'
Juniperus conferta
Juniperus horizontalis—and cultivars
Juniperus procumbens 'Nana'

FOR GROUND COVER—semi-prostrate
Juniperus x media 'Hetzii'
Juniperus x media 'Pfitzeriana'
Juniperus x media 'Pfitzeriana Aurea'
Juniperus virginiana 'Grey Owl'

FOR SHADE—no golden forms
in any genera should be used
Chamaecyparis obtusa cultivars
Chamaecyparis pisifera cultivars
Cryptomeria japonica and cultivars
Juniperus x media cultivars
Juniperus sabina and cultivars
Taxus baccata and cultivars

trouble free and because they fit in perfectly with the modern suburban garden. The shapes and forms of these fascinating plants provide a perennial interest, and contrary to some opinions, they do *not* look the same all the year round. It can again be seen from the colour photographs in the book, the differing shades of conifers in summer and winter. Add to this the fresh spring growth of pines and spruces and you have an everchanging pattern. We are lucky that the English climate is so amiable, for it enables us to grow a wide variety of plants. We are not usually "frozen in" during the winter and can therefore see plants that are willing to give a show. This applies particularly to conifers and other evergreens including heathers.

The summers are also not too hot, so therefore we can grow the golden foliage plants successfully. These tend to scorch in the United States for instance and are usually more prone to winter damage.

It is most effective to plant dwarf conifers in groups and a small border with nothing else but these plants can be most attractive. They do have a habit of growing however and may occasionally need thinning out! A good combination of shapes and colours can be achieved by selecting carefully, making sure to keep the dwarfer and slower growing types to the front of the border. This area can also be a useful "nursery" planting where one can put in small plants for a number of years before transplanting to a more spacious position.

The dwarfer kinds do not fit in well with large trees or conifers—they should be kept in scale and not made to look ridiculous. A background of larger conifers of course is not detrimental, but it is obvious that a 9m. *x Cupressocyparis leylandii* will not look right planted next to a *Picea mariana* 'Nana' at 30cm. high, but the same age.

Right:
This border in the Author's garden is planted with only dwarf and slow growing conifers providing interest the year round.

Above:
The larger conifers are more suited to a spacious setting where they will give the best display with their majestic forms.

Planting Soils & Care

Conifers are not generally fussy as to soil requirements and many, particularly the dwarf forms, can be grown in quite thin impoverished soil. However it will be necessary to qualify this by saying some conifers will do much better than others in such conditions. *Juniperus* are particularly adaptable and will survive and prosper where many other genera will not. On extremely chalky or limey soils *Juniperus* and *Taxus* can be relied upon to thrive and this gives more choice than might appear, as there is a wide range of plants represented in these genera.

Most gardens however will contain reasonable enough soil to grow most of the conifers shown in this book. The conifers one sees in gardens in the neighbourhood should give you some idea as to the potential. Many failures are cultural and not due to soil and if the following procedures are followed your plants should stand the best chance of success. *Obtain good quality plants.* Get a reasonable weed free tilth of soil to put the plants in. Make sure if planting in a border or in grass, that you have a large enough hole for the plant. Most conifers will not need fertilizers, but it can only do good to mix in a well balanced granular fertilizer with the soil prior to planting. For those lucky enough to obtain some well rotted compost or farmyard manure this dug or mixed with the soil will help give extra colour and vigour to the plant, help to conserve moisture in dry soils and help drainage in heavy soils.

Preparing for planting . . .   *Undercutting . . .*

MOVING AND PLANTING A CONIFER

Having prepared the planting hole, remove the container by cutting the polythene bag or gently knocking the plant from the pot. Make sure the plant is well watered beforehand. If the roots are wound round the pot like "clocksprings", tease them open to enable them to spread out and make fresh root. This should help the plant to stabilize itself against strong winds.

If the plant is a larger specimen and has come root wrapped in hessian drop the plant *first* into the hole then carefully remove the hessian, polythene or whatever container has been used. The hessian sacking can of course be left on to eventually rot, although it is usually advisable to remove if the plant has a reasonable rootball.

If the conifer is over 90cm. it may well need staking, particularly if it did not arrive with a large rootball, or has not got a good root system (see sketch 1, page 17). The stake should be inserted before filling in the hole so that root damage is avoided. Be sure when attaching the stake to the tree to use a proper tree tie, or otherwise ensure that the tree is well protected from chafing and damage to the bark. This can also be done by wrapping a piece of sacking around the trunk and tying with thick string around the stake and the sacking. The stake should be in the ground far enough to hold the tree firm against the wind. Do beware if you use polythene string to check it after some months to make sure it is not cutting into the trunk.

Fill in the hole around the roots with friable soil, taking care to gently lift the tree thereby easing the soil into all the spaces between the roots. Firm the soil according to its texture— if sandy (wet or dry) firm with your feet all around. If heavy (and particularly if wet) firm, but gently, otherwise waterlogging and bad drainage will occur, particularly in winter.

moving . . .   *planting . . .*

to make a good rootball . . .

wrapping to retain the rootball . . .

This will often result in losses or lack of growth particularly with *Chamaecyparis* species, and cultivars. Never leave the soil panned by footsteps, but make sure if on wet or heavy soil to prick up the surface after planting.

If the conifer is a fairly large one, it may pay, whether planting in autumn, winter or spring to make a fence lined with hessian sacking or polythene to protect the conifer from winter burn of scorch. Wind will do more damage than frost, although the combination of the two can kill newly transplanted conifers in exposed situations when not protected.

A point I think of most importance and one which is probably overlooked most frequently applies to conifers planted in grass or on lawns. At least a full 30cm. of turf should be cut out all round the base of the conifer and then kept completely clear of grass. As the plant grows so should the circle be kept clear, so if the diameter of the base of a conifer is 60cm. you need a 1·25m. diameter circle in

the grass. Many conifers are accustomed to a higher rainfall than is often available in England particularly in the South Eastern areas. For instance one has to travel to the west of Scotland or to the Lake District to realize how much taller and luxuriant many Conifers grow compared with Norfolk and Suffolk. Any help therefore that can be given to get your trees off to a good start the better will be the final specimen. The grass of course will not only prevent much of the moisture penetrating to the roots of the conifer, but if not kept in check will cause the bottom of the tree to lose its foliage. Once the foliage at the base becomes brown it will develop into a bare unsightly patch. This applies to most conifers, but particularly to *Chamaecyparis lawsoniana* cultivars, which will never break again from the base as will *Thuja plicata* for instance. Conifers can look unsightly and often do, but the main reason for them doing so is cultural and could often have been prevented.

in new position . . .

protecting if necessary.

MOVING AN ESTABLISHED CONIFER

Conifers can be moved reasonably safely at any time of the year as long as certain precautions are taken, although open ground plants may best be avoided from late May to early September. There is no problem in establishing a container grown plant bought at a garden centre as long as the normal planting instructions are followed and the plant is kept well watered during hot weather. However, if you are contemplating moving some of your larger specimen conifers it will pay to plan somewhat further ahead. Many specimens that have outgrown their present position in the garden should be root pruned the year before moving. This applies particularly to Junipers which tend to make a few roots and do not move so readily. Many of the *Thujas* and *Chamaecyparis* make a good rootball and therefore pruning may be not necessary, but doing so will nevertheless ensure a successful transplanting. Root pruning means cutting around the base of the conifer with a spade to sever some of the main roots, thereby encouraging the growth of the smaller fibrous roots from the centre of the plant. According to the size of the plant the roots should be pruned 15–46cm. from the central trunk (see sketch 2).

Of course when one starts moving a tree of over 2m, then the distance one prunes around will be much greater. Not that the average gardener is likely to move a conifer over that height without professional help.

One should prune at least to the depth of the spade and also undercut slightly if possible. If this is done in March or April the tree will have one full growing season to recover and be ready for the move the following autumn. However, if you feel the job must be done immediately or you have not got around to root pruning, it need not be disastrous to take a chance and move specimen trees, 5, 10 or 20 years old. I'm speaking regarding the latter period of the dwarf varieties of course. If conditions are dry, water the plant well before moving. Carefully dig around the plant to leave as much soil as possible attached to the root. Undercut with a sharp spade to make sure that all the roots are completely severed.

Then slide a sack or polythene bag under the rootball, so that all four corners can be held. If moving the tree some distance it will be necessary to wrap the sacking around the root and tie it tightly, using additional string if necessary in order to prevent the rootball from breaking up. Keeping the rootball intact if possible, lower the plant into the new position. If it is hot or windy weather the plant will need watering every evening and the foliage syringing. This will help to prevent the plant losing moisture faster than it can make new root to support itself. It may also pay to screen it as explained earlier.

If you do not wish to lose some specimen trees you have had with you for several years, it will pay to take the time and trouble to follow these instructions.

SITING

The siting of conifers is of some importance, particularly the golden foliage varieties. These should be in full sun to obtain the best colour although certain varieties do tend to winter burn, or scorch in extremely bright hot weather. This is of fairly rare occurrence and of course is not limited only to these types, but it is still worthwhile keeping any golden foliage variety out of a very draughty or exposed position. It has often been mentioned that if golden conifers colour better in the sun, blue or grey foliage plants colour better in semi-shade conditions. I have not really found this to be the case, although these forms will do well in such conditions.

PRUNING

For garden conifers pruning is sometimes necessary to improve shape. A conifer may produce two or more main leading shoots and to obtain a better shaped tree the best leader should be selected, the others cut out. Some prostrate or semi-prostrate Junipers may become overgrown and unshapely and need pruning back to make a more compact plant. Or of course, the ultimate, you may wish to make a hedge.

A CONIFER FOR A HEDGE

To my mind a good conifer hedge cannot be bettered; being evergreen of course it is able to protect a house or garden from the onslaught of winter weather and it can be most useful as a screen for privacy or to hide some unsightly view. A conifer hedge should be planted much the same as any other conifer, but spaced at 75–90cm. apart, using a line to keep it straight. A thorough preparation of the planting ground is again essential, using at least a 1·25m. width of trench. Although it may mean waiting a bit longer to achieve a good hedge, it is usually advisable to buy quite young plants for hedges. There are two reasons for this—for one, it allows the plants to establish a stronger root system necessary to withstand the wind; secondly, it is much less expensive!

A useful rule to follow when choosing a partilar hedge is to first decide how tall you wish it to grow. If you want an ultimate height of over 2·50m. then choose either *x Cupressocyparis leylandii* or *Thuja plicata*. The former is undoubtedly the best conifer hedging because of its easy establishment on a wide variety of soils and its quickness of growth. Both the species mentioned of course become large forest trees if left to grow untrimmed and therefore if you want a hedge at about 1·85m. then these are really too vigorous and will very likely resent being kept at this height indefinitely.

For a lower hedge it is better to choose something slower growing such as *Taxus baccata*, which may take much longer to reach 1·85m. than the two conifers previously mentioned, but will be much happier remaining at that height.

The plants will probably not need trimming for the first year or two, and then only at the sides until the required height is obtained. Thereafter it will need trimming at least once a year. July is probably the best month to trim a conifer hedge as it is less of a setback to the plant at that time. It has also made its first flush of growth and can be tidied up, leaving several months for the "cuts" to heal, giving a healthy but neat appearance through the winter.

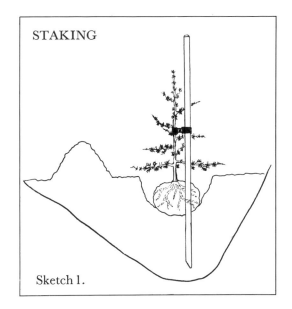

STAKING

Sketch 1.

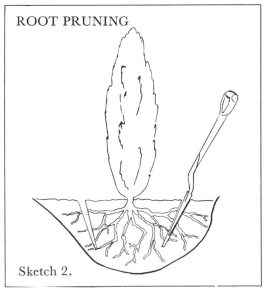

ROOT PRUNING

Sketch 2.

SPACING FOR
HEDGE PLANTING

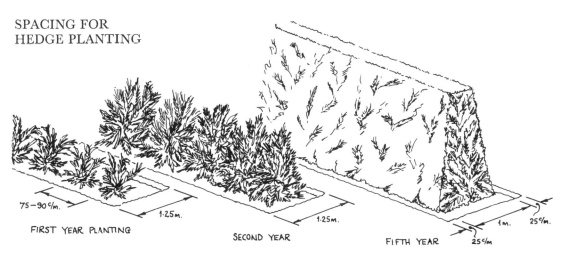

·75–90 c/m.

1·25m.

FIRST YEAR PLANTING

1·25m.

SECOND YEAR

FIFTH YEAR

25 c/m

1m.

25 c/m.

PROPAGATION OF CONIFERS

Conifers like other plants, are produced in various ways, from cuttings, seed and grafting. Many conifers are not difficult to root from cuttings, but nearly all take time, especially if no modern misting or heating equipment is available. To obtain the right material for a cutting in a cold frame, 1 to 2 year old ripened wood should be found, then detached from the "mother" plant with a "heel". This heel applies to the point where the cutting is severed from the main branch. The cutting should then be inserted in a half peat and half sharp sand mix, making sure to firm the cutting well into the mix. The rooting medium can be put in a seed tray or a clay pot, sunk in the ground in a northern aspect, where it can get light but not direct sunlight. The box can be surrounded by a brick or board frame and covered with a Dutch or polythene light or even more simply a pane of glass. The optimum time for propagation in this manner is probably August and September. Some of the cuttings may well be rooted by the late spring, but other types may not root for as

long as two years. The addition of some rooting hormone powder to the base of the cutting, prior to insertion in the medium, may well speed up the process.

The varieties of the species *Abies, Chamaecyparis, Cryptomeria, Juniperus, Picea, Taxus* and *Thuja* will generally root quite readily, but it is more difficult to get any results from varieties of *Cedrus, Cupressus, Pinus* and *Pseudotsuga*. The items that will not root from cuttings must be propagated by either seed or grafting. The larger growing Pines, such as *Pinus sylvestris* and *Pinus nigra* are usually grown from seed, as are the larger forms of *Cedrus, Picea, Cupressus* and *Pseudotsuga*. However any selected cultivar, such as *Cedrus atlantica* 'Aurea' or any dwarf forms must be grafted which is much more expensive and involved process—and generally beyond the scope of most amateur gardeners. It is of course clear that those plants which are either more difficult to propagate or slower growing will cost more money to buy from a nursery or garden centre.

Perhaps this is an appropriate place to point out the public's preoccupation with size in relation to value for money. This particularly

A five year old hedge of x Cupressocyparis leylandii

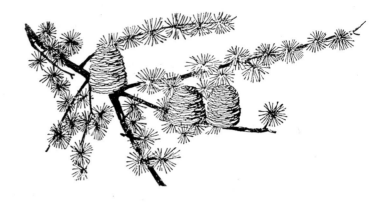

applies to the uneducated gardener, because any gardener who is familiar with plants and their rate of growth is aware of their value. Dwarf conifers come in for criticism on the fact that they will take at least 10 years to reach 1·25, 1·50 or 1·85m, and some really dwarf varieties will reach less than 80cm. in that time. What customers usually expect is that they can buy a young plant at 60–90cm. high and that it will grow 90cm. the next year and then stop! Conifers are not like animals or humans, in that they reach a certain height and size and when they become adult they stop growing (see our sketch). Conifers and trees of course do not behave in that manner; the rate of growth is controlled by their ultimate height. A conifer like *x Cupressocyparis leylandii* after 20 years will be likely to be 18m. or more, where *Picea glauca* 'Albertiana Conica' will be only 1·85m. or so. Divide the height by the years and you have your average rate of growth.

However, one of the great advantages with conifers is that one can find a plant for every purpose and this book will attempt in its colour plates particularly to prove that this is no idle boast!

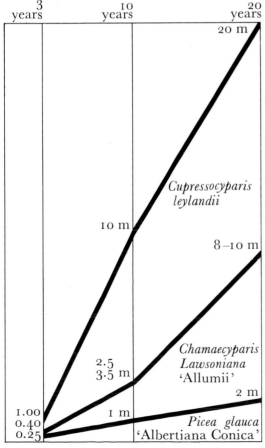

PESTS AND DISEASES

A short space should be devoted here to mention that like most other groups of plants, conifers have their enemies. Pests can be troublesome on certain conifers and our old friend *Picea glauca* 'Albertiana Conica' is one of these. Spider-mites can attack this and other conifers during late spring and early summer. Usually a close check from time to time will be all that is necessary, but it is nonetheless worth doing. These insects can suck at the fresh shoots of the plant and cause the needles to drop. Spider-mites are usually reddish in colour and visible to the naked eye. A spray over the affected plants with metasystox or some other systemic insecticide should clear these up. Spraying should be carried out preferably in the evening or on a dull day, otherwise scorching of young shoots can occur. It is also advisable to follow up this first spraying (before any damage is evident by the insects) with another two weeks later. This will ensure that any eggs which have since hatched out will be given the same treatment. There are several biting and sucking insects, many too small to be seen without a magnifying glass, which if given metasystox as described can be rendered harmless. This particular chemical is systemic, which means after being sprayed on the plant it becomes absorbed into the plant system and remains for at least a week to be sucked in by the offending insect, thereby destroying itself. For a more thorough examination of pests and diseases on conifers and the method of control, I cannot do better than recommend the "Manual of Cultivated Conifers" by Dr. B. K. Boom. This book has a considerable number of pages devoted to this subject, but one hopes that the average gardener will not find any need to refer in desperation to this chapter, excellent though it is!

Making the best use of Conifers

I have covered the basic uses of conifers in this preliminary text, but I feel it is necessary to stress as I do throughout the book that it is the *combination* of shapes, colours and forms of conifers together with other selected garden plants that can do so much to add beauty and interest to the garden. It will I hope become evident as you look through the colour pages that conifers have a hundred uses in a garden. The artificial dwarfing and pruning of trees, much better known as the art of Bonsai has not been referred to and will not be included in this book, but Bonsai culture does add yet a further dimension to the widespread uses of conifers.

The greens, blues, yellows and golds are so varied among the conifers that if carefully placed can highlight the garden scene both in summer and winter. In my opinion the combination of groupings of conifers and heathers is hard to beat. One can achieve a patchwork of form and colour, attractive the year round, giving a relaxing yet sophisticated garden scene. Although some considerable work may be necessary to establish this garden and some thought put to it, once planted, very little aftercare is needed.

There is not space in this book to go into any detail on heathers, but I would like to ask the reader to carefully look at the garden scenes in the colour section where conifers and heathers are planted together. Being generally low growing in habit and covering a flowering period of ten to eleven months, they can make a perfect setting for conifers. Heathers are good ground coverers and relatively trouble free although a careful study of specialist catalogues is worth the trouble before buying and planting. Ideas for planting plans can also be explored, but generally it is most effective to have large groupings of heathers interspaced with various single specimens of conifers. Peat should be added for the "Heaths"—*Calluna vulgaris* varieties and some other summer flowering varieties, and a peat mulch is always an advantage when first planting to keep down weeds, retain moisture and to enable the heathers to establish themselves. The result of planting young plants of both conifers and heathers together, can be best demonstrated by the colour picture on the opposite page. This was taken five years after planting and the natural blending of shapes and colours is already evident. Unfortunately space does not permit the use of planting plans in this book, but although they would be most useful for borders with a combination of conifers and heathers, for a purely conifer border there is such a wide range available that a more personal choice can easily be made. With a close study of eventual height and rate of growth an attractive Island Border can be created using only conifers.

It will generally be advisable however to plant only the dwarf and slow growing varieties, particularly in an Island Border, as otherwise they will soon look out of proportion to each other and the rest of the garden. An effective planting can be made using more than one of a kind. A grouping of 3 to 5 of one variety adds interest particularly when the plants are small. Enough space must be allowed between the plants to give growing room, and a careful choice to vary the upright and semi-prostrate types with the bushy and prostrate. Using these forms together with variations of colour and you should be able to create a border of continual interest for many years to come.

*Conifers and heathers
in the Author's garden,
at Bressingham.*

Synonyms

Some of the conifers in this book are also known under the following names;

ABIES page 24
Abies concolor 'Compacta' – *Abies concolor* var. *glauca* 'Compacta' – *Abies concolor* 'Glauca Compacta'
Abies delavayii var. *forrestii* – *Abies forrestii*
Abies lasiocarpa 'Compacta' – *Abies arizonica* 'Compacta'
Abies procera – *Abies nobilis*
ARAUCARIA page 29
Araucaria araucana – *Araucaria imbricata*
CALOCEDRUS – LIBOCEDRUS page 30
Calocedrus decurrens – *Libocedrus decurrens*
Calocedrus decurrens 'Aureovariegata' – *Libocedrus decurrens* 'Aureovariegata'
CEDRUS page 31
Cedrus libani 'Sargentii' – *Cedrus libani* 'Pendula Sargentii' – *Cedrus libani* 'Pendula'
CEPHALOTAXUS page 37
Cephalotaxus harringtonia var. *drupacea* – *Cephalotaxus drupacea*
CHAMAECYPARIS page 38
Chamaecyparis lawsoniana 'Columnaris' – *Chamaecyparis lawsoniana* 'Columnaris Glauca'
Chamaecyparis lawsoniana 'Ellwood's White' – *Chamaecyparis lawsoniana* 'Ellwoodii Variegata'
Chamaecyparis lawsoniana 'Erecta' – *Chamaecyparis lawsoniana* 'Erecta Viridis'
Chamaecyparis lawsoniana 'Lanei' – *Chamaecyparis lawsoniana* 'Lane'
Chamaecyparis lawsoniana 'Nana Albospica' – *Chamaecyparis lawsoniana* 'Nana Alba'
Chamaecyparis lawsoniana 'Pygmaea Argentea' – *Chamaecyparis lawsoniana* 'Backhouse Silver'
Chamaecyparis lawsoniana 'Spek' – *Chamaecyparis lawsoniana* 'Glauca Spek'
Chamaecyparis nootkatensis 'Lutea' – *Chamaecyparis nootkatensis* 'Aurea'
Chamaecyparis obtusa – *Retinospora obtusa*
Chamaecyparis obtusa 'Intermedia' – *Chamaecyparis obtusa* 'Nana Intermedia'
Chamaecyparis obtusa 'Kosteri' – *Chamaecyparis obtusa* 'Nana Kosteri'
Chamaecyparis pisifera – *Retinospora pisifera*
Chamaecyparis pisifera 'Boulevard' – *Chamaecyparis pisifera* 'Cyano viridis'
Chamaecyparis thyoides 'Andelyensis' – *Chamaecyparis thyoides* 'Leptoclada'
CUPRESSUS page 69
Cupressus glabra – *Cupressus arizonica* – *Cupressus arizonica* bonita
JUNIPERUS page 73
Juniperus chinensis 'Japonica' – *Juniperus chinensis* 'Japonica Oblonga'
Juniperus chinensis 'Kaizuka' – *Juniperus chinensis* 'Torulosa' – *Juniperus chinensis* var. *torulosa*
Juniperus communis var. *depressa* – *Juniperus canadensis*
Juniperus communis 'Hibernica' – *Juniperus hibernica*
Juniperus communis 'Repanda' – *Juniperus communis* 'Repandens'
Juniperus conferta – *Juniperus littoralis*
Juniperus davurica 'Expansa' – *Juniperus chinensis* 'Parsonsii'
Juniperus horizontalis 'Wiltonii' – *Juniperus horizontalis* 'Blue Rug'
Juniperus x media – see notes on page 82
Juniperus x media 'Blaauw' – *Juniperus chinensis* 'Blaauw' – *Juniperus chinensis* 'Blaauw's Variety'
Juniperus x media 'Hetzii' – *Juniperus chinensis* 'Hetzii'
Juniperus x media 'Old Gold' – *Juniperus chinensis* 'Old Gold'
Juniperus x media 'Pfitzeriana' – *Juniperus chinensis* 'Pfitzeriana'
Juniperus x media 'Pfitzeriana Aurea' – *Juniperus chinensis* 'Pfitzeriana Aurea'
Juniperus x media 'Plumosa Aurea' – *Juniperus chinensis* 'Plumosa Aurea'
Juniperus procumbens 'Nana' – *Juniperus procumbens* 'Bonin Isles'
Juniperus recurva 'Embley Park' – *Juniperus recurva* 'Viridis'
Juniperus sargentii – *Juniperus chinensis* var. *sargentii*
Juniperus scopulorum 'Skyrocket' – *Juniperus virginiana* 'Skyrocket'
LARIX page 92
Larix decidua – *Larix europaea*
Larix kaempferi – *Larix leptolepis*

PICEA page 95
Picea abies – Picea excelsa
Picea mariana 'Nana' – *Picea nigra* 'Pygmaea'
Picea orientalis 'Aurea' – *Picea orientalis* 'Aureospicata'
Picea pungens 'Globosa' – *Picea pungens* 'Glauca Globosa'
Picea pungens 'Prostrata' – *Picea pungens* 'Glauca Prostrata'
PINUS page 106
Pinus griffithii - *Pinus wallichiana* - *Pinus excelsa*
Pinus mugo – Pinus mughus – Pinus montana
Pinus nigra – Pinus nigra austriaca
Pinus nigra maritima – Pinus laricio – Pinus calabrica
Pinus sylvestris 'Watereri' – *Pinus sylvestris* 'Pumila'
PSEUDOTSUGA page 121
Pseudotsuga menziesii – Pseudotsuga taxifolia – Pseudotsuga douglasii – Pseudotsuga glauca
Pseudotsuga menziesii 'Fletcheri' – *Pseudotsuga glauca* 'Fletcheri'
SEQUOIA page 123
Sequoia sempervirens 'Adpressa' – *Sequoia sempervirens* 'Albospica'
SEQUOIADENDRON - **SEQUOIA** page 124
Sequoiadendron giganteum - *Sequoia gigantea* - *Sequoia wellingtonia*
TAXUS page 126
Taxus baccata 'Standishii' - *Taxus baccata* 'Fastigiata Standishii'
THUJA – THUYA page 132
Thuja occidentalis 'Holmstrup' – *Thuja occidentalis* 'Holmstrupensis' – *Thuja occidentalis* 'Holmstrupii'
Thuja occidentalis 'Wareana Lutescens' – *Thuja occidentalis* 'Lutescens'
Thuja orientalis – Biota orientalis
Thuja orientalis 'Juniperoides' – *Thuja orientalis* 'Decussata'
Thuja orientalis 'Rosedalis' – *Thuja orientalis* 'Rosedalis Compacta'
Thuja plicata – Thuja lobbii
Thuja plicata 'Rogersii' – *Thuja plicata* 'Rogersii Aurea'
THUJOPSIS *dolobrata* – **THUYA** *dolobrata* page 140
TSUGA page 140
Tsuga canadensis 'Bennett' – *Tsuga canadensis* 'Bennett's Minima'
Tsuga canadensis 'Cole' – *Tsuga canadensis* 'Cole's Prostrate'
Tsuga canadensis 'Horsford' – *Tsuga canadensis* 'Horsford's Dwarf'

Explanation of symbols

To help in identifying the habit and rate of growth of each conifer in the list, letters are given as follows:
D. *Dwarf.*   M. *Medium.*   L. *Large tree.*
Against each variety is shown the habit of the plant by means of a symbol:

Columnar.   Pendulous.   Conical.

After the first letter is given the height after 10 years, i.e. M. 90cm.–1·20m. Following this the Ultimate Height is given, i.e. U.H.

3–3·60m. For Prostrate and Semi-Prostrate forms the spread is shown as S. and Ultimate Spread as U.S.
A complete example is as follows:

Chamaecyparis pisifera 'Boulevard'

D. 90cm.–1·20m. U.H. 3–3·60m.

The metric system is used as a form of measurement throughout this book and it must be stressed that with so many variable factors determining growth, all heights given must be approximate.

23

ABIES

Most of the Abies are large growing or forest trees, although there is one species that comes into the dwarf or slow growing category. The "Silver Firs" as they are known, usually have a symetrical outline, columnar or conical. They will, like many other forest trees, lose their bottom branches as they get older. The trunk very rarely forks and the side branches are arranged in tiers.

Most Abies species are green or blue-grey in appearance with the underneath of the leaves showing grey or white. The taller forest trees can be very imposing and majestic. Many of the species—and there are about 40 of them in cultivation—are not really suitable as garden plants, but there will always be room for some of the slower growing and prostrate forms. For a woodland site the larger types will add interest and variety to the planting. They can be slow to establish but will then grow quite rapidly. All the larger growing Abies have the added attraction of bearing cones quite freely, some species when quite young. The Abies species all hold their cones upwards on top of the branches, which distinguish them from the Piceas, which have their cones hanging underneath.

Abies balsamea 'Hudsonia'. A specimen aged 15 years.

Abies balsamea 'Hudsonia'

D. 20–30cm.   U.H. 60–90cm.

This plant is one of the few good dwarf *Abies*, making a compact but almost prostrate shrub. The "Balsam Fir" *A. balsamea*, mainly found in North America reaches 20–30m. and this pygmy form of the species was discovered in the White Mountains of New Hampshire. It has deep glossy green leaves and like most of the *Abies* species, most attractive when making new spring growth.

It is a very useful rock garden plant, slow growing and very hardy.

Abies concolor 'Compacta' in early summer.

Abies concolor 'Compacta'

M. 60–90cm.   U.H. 1·80–3·00m.

This rather rare but very beautiful form is also known under the name *A. concolor* var. *glauca* 'Compacta'. It is somewhat irregular in shape with a very glaucous tinge to the foliage, particularly in the period of new growth, May to July. This plant will only be obtainable from specialists but is well worth looking for.

Abies concolor, a 10 year old specimen.

Abies concolor

L. 2·25m.   U.H. 25–50m.
The height of this and some other large growing conifers will vary quite considerably in different localities, mainly on account of depth of soil and rainfall. The "Colorado White Fir" retains its lower branches longer than some other species which adds to its usefulness as a specimen plant. It has quite large cones turning from green to a purplish tinge.

Abies delavayii var. *forestii.* – *A detailed study of the underside of the leaves.*

Abies delavayi var. *forestii*

M. 1·80–2·40m.   U.H. 7–9m.

This variety of *A. delavayii* is one that should be better known and more widely planted. It has reddish young shoots, most distinctive leaves, dark green above and a very silvery-white underneath. The tree cones early growing to about 8–10cm. in length, and a startling bluish-black. For the garden with space and the gardener who is looking for something different this plant is worth searching for.

Abies grandis

L. 3·00–3·60m.   U.H. 80–100m.

This is one of the giant forest trees imported during the last century from the Pacific North West of the U.S.A. It makes rapid growth when established, preferring moist but well drained soils. It grows very successfully in this country, but could not really be classed as a garden conifer. It has a glossy green foliage, with white bands underneath the leaves. This tree, and other giant forest trees have a certain fascination as adult specimens, being somewhat similar to whales and elephants in that they achieve such tremendous stature!

Abies grandis. A 10 year old specimen.

Abies koreana with its striking cones.

Abies koreana

L. 1·80–2·40m.   U.H. 15m.

The "Korean Fir" has a neat looking appearance and is a useful plant for the larger garden. The foliage, glossy green on top, whitish beneath, is attractive the year round, but one of the most interesting points of this tree is that it has purple cones at a very young age. On many species of *Abies* the cones do not come until the plant is a considerable age, and then because one has to view them looking up at a distance, they are often missed by the unobservant. This is not likely to happen with *A. koreana* as the effect is quite startling.

Abies lasiocarpa

M. 1·20–1·80m.   U.H. 20–25m.

This is normally a slow growing conifer commonly known as the "Alpine Fir". Its erect branches and pale grey-green foliage makes it an attractive tree.

Abies lasiocarpa 'Compacta'.

Abies nordmanniana.

Abies lasiocarpa 'Compacta'

D. 60–90cms.   U.H. 1·80–2·40m

This form also passes under the name of *A. arizonica* 'Compacta' in some catalogues, but the name given here is now ascertained to be the correct one. This is a slow growing and irregular shaped plant with unusual greyish-green foliage. It is particularly attractive when making fresh summer growth in May and June.

Abies nordmanniana

L. 3–4m.   U.H. 50–60m.

The "Caucasian Fir" is obviously unsuitable for all but the largest gardens, but is nevertheless of great ornamental value. It has horizontal branches arranged in tiers and clothed to the ground. The winter buds are an attractive reddish-brown and the leaves a glossy green, marked underneath with two white bands. It is an adaptable and disease resistant species.

Abies pinsapo

L. 1·80–2·40m.   U.H. 20–25m.

The "Spanish Fir" is a reliable *Abies* for most types of soils and will do well in chalk. It has dark green leaves and differs from most other *Abies* by its broadly pyramidal shape and rather close rigid-looking foliage. The cones are cylindrical and purple-brown when young. Because of its adaptability this is one of the most useful of the *Abies* species.

Abies pinsapo.

Abies pinsapo 'Glauca'.

Abies pinsapo 'Glauca'

L. 1·80–2·40m.   U.H. 20–25m.

This cultivar is more widely grown on the European continent than the British Isles, but deserves to be better known on account of its attractive blue-grey leaves. It makes an ideal specimen tree where space can be allowed for its development.

Abies procera

L. 2·40–3·00m.   U.H. 60–90m.

This slender conical tree is known with good reason as "The Noble Fir". It is also listed in some catalogues by the name *A. nobilis*, hence the common name. Again rather large as a garden conifer, but good for woodland plant- ing with bluish-green foliage and large cones. It does not like thin chalky soils. *A. procera* 'Glauca' is even bluer in appearance and there are one or two prostrate forms of this plant available in specialist's catalogues which are most attractive if sometimes a bit lax in habit.

Araucaria araucana. — This specimen in Norfolk, England, is well over 100 years old.

ARAUCARIA

This very distinctive genus has given us one hardy species which is widely known and planted.

Araucaria araucana

L. 1·20–1·50m.   U.H. 25–30m.

This is the unusual looking "Monkey Puzzle" tree. Although quite slow growing it will eventually make quite a large tree. It has a fairly open habit with thick dark green branches, the leaves arranged in spirals along the length of the branch. These are a deep glossy green and the pointed outer edges quite sharp. It is very hardy and grows successfully in moist soils.

With age it becomes more round topped and the bottom branches begin to fall off. When that happens it's time to start thinking about planting another young specimen!

CALOCEDRUS

To be botanically correct this genus should be listed under Calocedrus , but as the most commonly used name for the species mentioned below is Libocedrus and is listed as such in both Mr. H. J. Welch's and P. den Ouden and Dr. B. K. Boom's books, I propose to follow suit.

Calocedrus decurrens

L. 2–2·5m.   U.H. 30–35m.

The "Incense Cedar" is a very distinct and beautiful tree and although eventually becoming large it is sufficiently slow in growth to be a useful garden conifer. It makes a broad column of rich green, the colour being held throughout the year. The branches are short, the flattened foliage sprays fan-shaped. This species retains its bottom branches even on old specimens, a point in its favour as a garden plant. For a very large garden a grouping of three or more plants can be most effective especially where they can be viewed from some distance.

Calocedrus decurrens 'Aureovariegata'

M. 2m.   U.H. 15–20m.

This cultivar is slower growing than the species, having similar habit and foliage, but the leaves are irregularly splashed with gold, making a most attractive and ornamental tree.

Calocedrus decurrens 'Aureovariegata'
This fine specimen is about 20 years old.

Calocedrus decurrens. – An old specimen of the "Incense Cedar".

CEDRUS

The "Cedars" although not a large genus, include some excellent garden conifers and are grown widely because of their adaptability and ease of culture. They include some very large species which are familiar to the observant in nearly every corner of the British Isles. They generally prefer a well drained loamy soil, but will grow on heavy clay if not too wet. With age some of the larger Cedars change their habit from conical to flat-topped. The leaves are arranged in little tufts along the branches and branchlets, spirally on the young shoots. The species have large barrel-shaped cones, standing upright and nestling in the branches. Unfortunately the cones do not appear until the trees are some age.

Cedrus atlantica 'Aurea'. – A 15 year old plant.

Cedrus atlantica 'Glauca' at about 15 years...

Cedrus atlantica 'Aurea'

M. 1–2m.   U.H. 3–5m.
This cultivar is much more commonly seen on the continent than in England. It is not very robust in habit and very much slower than the species. The leaves are a golden yellow. A nice specimen when seen at its best.

Cedrus atlantica 'Glauca'

L. 3–4m.   U.H. 35–40m.
This "Blue Cedar" or "Atlas Cedar" is one of the most beautiful of all conifers. It is a selected form of *C. atlantica* and like the species eventually becomes a very imposing tree. It is really too large for a small suburban garden as it needs space to show off its talents as a specimen plant. Bluish forms do occur from seed but most plants obtainable will have been propagated by grafting. It will therefore need careful staking to train the main leading shoot to grow vertically. Once it is established and the leading shoot reaches over 1·85m. it should be on its way without further assistance.
This is a plant worth siting carefully and looking after as it will repay handsomely for attention given in years to come.

Cedrus atlantica 'Glauca Pendula'

L. 1·50–2·20m.   U.H. 5–10m.

This plant is not often seen in England. It has the same bluish-white foliage of the previous cultivar but its branches fall downwards from the main trunk giving it an umbrella-like appearance. It must be trained upwards in its early years, otherwise it will become a prostrate plant.

Cedrus deodara 'Pendula'. – If not trained upwards in early years this would be a prostrate plant.

... and what it could be like at 100 years old. — This imposing specimen in Bagatelle France is 35 metres high.

Cedrus deodara. — This 6 year old plant is seen making fresh spring growth.

Cedrus brevifolia

M. 60–90cm.   U.H. 10–12m.
The "Cyprian Cedar" is a very slow growing
species with small bluish green or green
leaves, making a small to medium-sized tree.

Cedrus deodara

L. 3–5m.   U.H. 50m.
The "Himalayan Cedar" or "Deodar Cedar"
is a very beautiful and graceful tree. It was introduced to England from its native habitat,
the Himalayan mountains in the early 1800s
and has since become a part of our landscape
along with *C. libani* and *C. atlantica. C. deodara*
differs from the other species in its drooping
tips and arching leader. As the species is
grown from seed it can vary in its greyish
hues, with sometimes a touch of silver on the
leaves.
In some parts of Western Europe the Deodar Cedar is not completely hardy, but it is
rarely damaged by our winters. It is an ideal
specimen tree but room for expansion should
be allowed, for although a slow starter after
transplanting, it soon puts on height and
width.

rus deodara. — A 20 year old specimen.

rus deodara 'Aurea'.
e foliage is more golden in early summer.

Cedrus deodara 'Aurea'

M. 1·20–1·50m.   U.H. 3–5m.
The "Golden Deodar Cedar" is much slower
growing but will vary in ultimate height and
rate of growth according to climate. It is not
so hardy as the species. The leaves turn a
golden yellow in spring, losing this colour
slightly through the autumn and winter. Although most attractive when well grown this
can be a disappointment in some situations.

Cedrus libani

L. 1·80–2·40m.   U.H. 25–40m.
The "Cedar of Lebanon" is famous for its historical and biblical associations; the oldest recorded specimen still in cultivation in England dates back to about 1638. *C. libani* is not now planted much having been somewhat overtaken in popularity by *C. deodara*. This species is conical when young, becoming characteristically flat topped with age. Its leaves vary from bright to dark green. It is of slower growth than *C. atlantica* with more numerous branches.

Cedrus libani 'Nana'. – *This plant is over 20 years old.*
Cedrus libani 'Sargentii'.
Ideal for planting near a wall.

Cedrus libani 'Nana'

M. 60–90cm.   U.H. 5–6m.
This is a slow growing cultivar of compact and dense habit. It has branches clothed with tufts of bright green leaves.

Cedrus libani 'Sargentii'

P. S. 60–90cm.   U.S. 3–4m.
This is a most attractive conifer for a large rock garden or a bank. It is slow growing with a true weeping habit. It can be trained upwards when young to a required height and will then in time form a rounded bush. It can be used to its best advantage hanging over a wall or a small rock outcrop. If not used or trained in the right position it can sprawl most untidily. With this cultivar and many other conifers the use to which they are put and the way they are cultivated are all important.

Cephalotaxus harringtonia var. *drupacea*.

CEPHALOTAXUS

This is a small genus closely allied to the Taxus family and in appearance resemble large leaved "Yews".

The few species and cultivars are not widely known but are all shrubby in nature, growing well in shade and on chalky soils.

Cephalotaxus harringtonia var. *drupacea*

D. 60–90cm.   U.H. 2–3m.

This variety has two interesting common names "The Cow's tail Pine" and the "Japanese Plum Yew", the first perhaps descriptive of its branches and the second of its fruits which are olive-green. The plant itself has light green leaves. There is a form of *C. harringtonia* resembling the "Irish Yew" both in its habit and in the colour of its deep green leaves called *C. harringtonia* 'Fastigiata'.

CHAMAECYPARIS

This is one of the most widely grown and planted genera in Western Europe, although none of the six species are native to that part of the world. They come originally from North America, Japan and Formosa and have produced a very wide range of cultivars, varying considerably in height, habit and colour.

The Chamaecyparis or "False Cypress" is often referred to under its old name Cupressus, but the latter name covers a different and distinct group of species. Most of the Chamaecyparis species and cultivars grow more successfully where there is adequate moisture and good drainage. They dislike exposed positions and drying winds and can sometimes be difficult to transplant because of this reason. However, there are so many good garden plants among the Chamaecyparis that a little extra after-care is well worthwhile.

Chamaecyparis lawsoniana

L. 2·50–3m.   U.H. 35m.

The "Lawson Cypress" was introduced to Scotland just over a hundred years ago, and both it and its many cultivars are now widely planted. The species becomes a very large tree in time and is not now often planted as a specimen—selected cultivars usually fulfilling this function. It does however make a very useful screen or hedge if planted and cared for properly. *C. lawsoniana* like its many cultivars dislikes grass growing around its base. It tends to go bare and will not recover its foliage. Also when trimming as a hedge one should not cut into the old wood, because new shoots will not appear as they do with *Thuja plicata* or *Cupressocyparis leylandii*. *C. lawsoniana* and its cultivars will sometimes winterburn in an exposed position, particularly just after transplanting.

Following is a selection of the most distinct and useful cultivars of *C. lawsoniana*—there are far too many in cultivation to mention them all.

Chamaecyparis lawsoniana 'Albovariegata'

M. 1·20—1·50m.   U.H. 5–7m.

This cultivar has green foliage with the tips of the branches flecked with white. It can be a slightly unstable form with some plants appearing to have more white than others.

Chamaecyparis lawsoniana 'Allumii'

M. 1·80–2·20m.   U.H. 10–15m.

This is one of the most popular of the bluish foliage "Lawson" cultivars. It has a fairly compact habit, making a good specimen plant.

Chamaecyparis lawsoniana 'Albovariegata'.

Chamaecyparis lawsoniana 'Allumii'.

Chamaecyparis lawsoniana 'Columnaris'. — One of the most effective of conifers for the garden.

Chamaecyparis lawsoniana 'Columnaris'

M. 1·80–2·50m.   U.H. 7–9m.

In my opinion this is one of the best of the "Lawsons". It forms a narrow pillar of bluish-grey, most effective for landscaping and for a focal point in the garden. Some forms appear to be much narrower in outline than others.

Chamaecyparis lawsoniana 'Ellwoodii'. – *A beautiful 12 year old specimen.*

Chamaecyparis lawsoniana 'Ellwoodii'

D. 1·80–2m.   U.H. 4·50–6m.

Probably this is the most popular conifer grown in England. One sees many "culti-variants" of 'Ellwoodii' but although perhaps slightly different in habit they all have close grey-green foliage with more of a bluish hue in winter. It is a popular plant for tub planting, for rockeries and as a garden specimen. There is a "sport" of 'Ellwoodii' known as 'Chilworth Silver' which would appear to have a more silvery-blue cast to its foliage.

C. l. 'Ellwood's Gold' is another "sport" with the same habit but somewhat slower in growth. It is not a gold in the true sense of the word but the tips of the branchlets are tinged yellow, particularly in the summer, giving the plant a most pleasing appearance.

One can gather that 'Ellwoodii' altogether is quite a "sporting" cultivar as there is also a white variegated plant in cultivation called 'Ellwood's White'.

Chamaecyparis lawsoniana 'Gimbornii'

Chamaecyparis lawsoniana 'Erecta'.
An 8 year old plant.

Chamaecyparis lawsoniana 'Ellwood's Gold'. — *A 5 year old plant in early spring.*

Chamaecyparis lawsoniana 'Erecta'

M.–L. 1·80–2·25m.   U.H. 12–15m.

The long deep green and erect branches of this cultivar give it its name, as they branch from the base of the tree to give it its flame-shape. It does tend to go a little bare at the bottom as a specimen and if the branches are not tied they will open up by snow. As it ages it becomes a more broad based tree, eventually reaching a considerable size, especially in areas of high rainfall. This cultivar is also known under the name 'Erecta Viridis'.

Chamaecyparis lawsoniana 'Fletcheri'. — *A 15 year old plant.*

Chamaecyparis lawsoniana 'Fletcheri'

M. 2·25m.   U.H. 5–7m.

Another popular "Lawson" cultivar, particularly in England. It is broadly columnar with soft grey-green foliage and although similar to 'Ellwoodii' it quite quickly becomes too large for the rock garden, a situation for which it is commonly recommended.

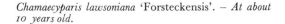

Chamaecyparis lawsoniana 'Forsteckensis'

D. 25–30cm.   U.H. 1m. x U.S. 1·5m.
This is a very old cultivar, the true form of which is a very congested globular bush, very slow growing with greyish-green foliage. From within the plant it pushes up new shoots which twist and curve in several directions. There appear to be one or two more open growing forms which become much larger.

Chamaecyparis lawsoniana 'Gimbornii'

D. 25–30cm.   U.H. 1m.
Although this cultivar is similar to 'Minima Glauca' it makes a much tighter neater plant, with foliage blue-green and the tips purplish. It is one of those plants that tend to "grow on you".

Chamaecyparis lawsoniana 'Green Pillar'

M. 1·50–1·80m.   U.H. 10–12m.
Although this cultivar is similar in shape to 'Erecta' it is a much brighter green and does not apparently damage from snowfall and so must be classed as a better garden plant, even though not so well known.

Chamaecyparis lawsoniana 'Green Pillar'.

Chamaecyparis lawsoniana 'Intertexta'

L. 1·80–2·25m.   U.H. 15–20m.

This becomes quite a large tree and can only be recommended for a situation where space is available. It has an open ascending habit but the branchlets attractively droop, giving the tree a graceful appearance. Whilst young however, the tree, though distinct does not look particularly desirable.

Chamaecyparis lawsoniana 'Kilmacurragh'

M. 1·5–2m.   U.H. 12–15m.

A narrow column of green would best describe this cultivar. The branches are short and semi-erect and the appearance is somewhat similar to *C. l.* 'Columnaris' in which it must be equal to its "architectural" possibilities.

Chamaecyparis lawsoniana 'Knowfieldensis'

D.–M. 50–60cm. x S. 1m.
U.H. 1m. x U.S. 2m.

There is a certain amount of confusion in some minds as to what is the true 'Knowfieldensis' as both 'Nidiformis', which becomes much larger and 'Tamariscifolia', which is a much deeper sea green, have often been put under the same label. The true plant would appear to have much smaller and flatter sprays overlapping each other. It is a more dwarf compact shrub than either of the other two with light green foliage, slightly glaucous beneath.

Chamaecyparis lawsoniana 'Lanei'. – *This photograph was taken in England in the middle of winter.*

Chamaecyparis lawsoniana 'Lanei'

M. 1·80–2·25m.   U.H. 10–15m.

One of the best "Golden Lawsons" for both summer and winter colour and a "must" for the medium to large garden. Like all golden conifers it needs an open south facing position and on its southern side will give its best colour. In association with blue and green conifers of similar rates of growth this cultivar can be most effective.

Chamaecyparis lawsoniana 'Lutea'.

Chamaecyparis lawsoniana 'Lutea'

M. 2–2·50m.   U.H. 10–13m.
This popular cultivar was first introduced almost a hundred years ago. It is columnar in shape and its branches have an open graceful appearance. It keeps a good winter colour, but is less bright than 'Lanei'.

Chamaecyparis lawsoniana 'Maas'

M. 2·50–3m.   U.H. 10–12m.

A broadly conical, relatively fast growing "Lawson", not much grown in England, being of fairly recent introduction in Holland. The foliage is an attractive yellow green.

Chamaecyparis lawsoniana 'Minima Aurea'

D. 25–35cm.   U.H. 1·25–1·60m.

If there is one conifer which must be classed as truly outstanding for a small garden it is this one. Although a very slow growing plant, its bright yellow and tightly packed foliage makes an ideal year round specimen. It is ideal for the small heather garden or rock garden and is a real joy in winter, being almost brighter in colour than in the summer. *C. l.* 'Aurea Densa' was raised at the same nursery, W. H. Rogers and Son, Eastleigh, Hampshire, in a batch of seedlings. This cultivar is indistinguishable from 'Minima Aurea' in its young stages, but eventually becomes a much tighter and more rounded shape. Both are worth obtaining although a long wait may be necessary to appreciate the difference!

Chamaecyparis lawsoniana 'Minima Aurea', *aged about 7 years.*

Chamaecyparis lawsoniana 'Minima Glauca'

D. 25–30cm.   U.H. 1·25–1·50m.

This is a very slow growing rounded bush with no leader and one should not be confused by the name 'Glauca' being applied to it. The plant is more of a sea green with very little blue evident. It is one of the most popular dwarf cultivars. *C. l.* 'Nana' is often wrongly labelled as 'Minima Glauca', the difference being that 'Nana' has normally a definite leader and a thick central trunk and more horizontally held branches. As young plants they are very difficult to distinguish.

Chamaecyparis lawsoniana 'Nana Albospica'

D. 50–75cm.   U.H. 1·90–2·25m.

This cultivar which has the appearance of being snow-covered in summer should in my opinion be more widely grown. It will not like a very exposed position but otherwise seems quite hardy. It is light green inside the plant and generally has a creamy appearance, but much whiter when summer growth commences. A very useful addition to the colour range of conifers.

Chamaecyparis lawsoniana 'Nana Albospica'. – *During most of the summer the foliage becomes much whiter.*

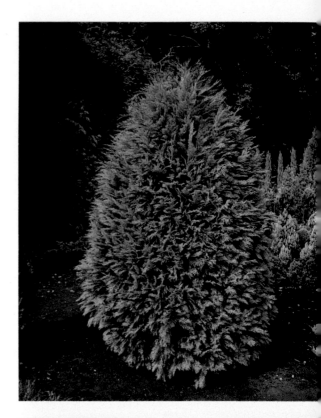

Chamaecyparis lawsoniana 'Pembury Blue'

M. 2–3m.   U.H. 7–10m.
Perhaps the bluest of the "Lawson" cultivars, this makes a conical tree with silvery-blue foliage. Of fairly recent introduction this deserves to be better known.

Chamaecyparis lawsoniana 'Pottenii'

M. 2–2·5m.   U.H. 10–15m.
Although an old cultivar this is still popular and a good garden plant. It has feathery, delicate looking foliage of light green, very bushy in appearance and soft to the touch. It can be a little prone to wind damage and great care should be taken when transplanting to give protection against drying winds.

Chamaecyparis lawsoniana 'Pottenii'.

48

Chamaecyparis lawsoniana 'Pygmaea Argentea'

D. 20–30cm.   U.H. 1m.
Another cultivar which should be much more widely grown as it has the advantage of an excellent winter and summer colour. It is of very slow growth but is attractive even as a small plant with its silvery-white tips capping the bluish-green foliage. These tips can burn unfortunately through extremes of sun and frost but nevertheless it needs a fully exposed position to obtain the best colour. The cultivar 'Backhouse Silver' would appear to be identical with this.

Chamaecyparis lawsoniana 'Pygmaea Argentea'. — *A 5 year old plant in summer.*

Chamaecyparis lawsoniana 'Spek'.

Chamaecyparis lawsoniana 'Spek'

M. 1·80–2·20m.   U.H. 7–10m.
Of Dutch origin, this is also known under the name 'Glauca Spek'. It is in many ways similar to 'Pembury Blue' but without quite so much silver in the foliage. A very attractive cultivar.

Chamaecyparis lawsoniana 'Stewartii'

M. 2·5–4m.   U.H. 10-14m.
This cultivar together with 'Lutea' and 'Lanei' is the most popular of the medium sized golden "Lawsons". It is much more of a gold than a yellow becoming more of a yellow-green in the winter, and not so bright as the other two cultivars mentioned.

Chamaecyparis
lawsoniana 'Stewartii'
at about 7 years old.

Chamaecyparis lawsoniana 'Tamariscifolia'. The bright green foliage is most attractive in winter.

Chamaecyparis lawsoniana 'Triomf van Boskoop'.

Chamaecyparis lawsoniana 'Tamariscifolia'

S.P. 1m. x S. 1·5m. U.H. 2–3m. x U.S. 4–5m. This was referred to under 'Knowfieldensis' under which name this cultivar is sometimes seen. It becomes a medium to large sized bush in time. It is a perfect foil for golden foliaged plants with its rich sea-green colour, held throughout the winter months. The branchlets are fan-like, twisting and overlapping, the habit spreading, semi-prostrate when young but becoming umbrella-like when older.

Chamaecyparis lawsoniana 'Triomf van Boskoop'

M–L. 3–4m.   U.H. 15–18m.
In my opinion this old but still popular cultivar has been superseded by other glaucous forms 'Pembury Blue' and 'Spek'. It has coarse open sprays of grey-blue and really needs trimming to obtain a more dense and attractive appearance.

Chamaecyparis lawsoniana 'Westermannii'

M. 2·5–3m.   U.H. 7–10m.
Although an old cultivar, having been introduced in Holland as long ago as 1880, this has not become particularly popular in England. It is quite distinctive with large light yellow sprays which are almost pendulous.

Chamaecyparis lawsoniana 'Winston Churchill'

M. 1·5–2m.   U.H. 6–8m.
This is one of the best golden "Lawsons" and can be compared in colour most closely to 'Lanei'. It is relatively slow growing but maintains its rich golden yellow colour throughout the year, and on this account alone must stand as a worthy garden plant.

Chamaecyparis lawsoniana 'Wissellii'

M. 2·5–3m.   U.H. 9–12m.
This cultivar is quite distinct from most of the other "Lawsons" with its close bluish-green leaves and upward twisting branches. It has the added attraction of being covered with red "flowers" in spring.

Chamaecyparis lawsoniana 'Westermannii'.

Chamaecyparis lawsoniana 'Wissellii'.

A conifer and heather garden on the large scale.
This photograph was taken in March
in the Heather Garden at the
Royal Horticultural Society Gardens
Wisley, England.

Chamaecyparis nootkatensis

L. 3–4m.   U.H. 30–40m.
The "Nootka Cypress" is not particularly well known although it is a very handsome tree. It comes from the same region as *Chamaecyparis lawsoniana*, Western North America. With age it becomes more pendulous in habit, making a beautiful specimen tree. The foliage is a dull green and coarse to the touch with a distinctive smell. This species really becomes too large to be considered for anywhere except a large garden where space is no problem. The species and its cultivars are extremely hardy and adaptable.

Chamaecyparis nootkatensis. – A 10 year old plant.

Chamaecyparis nootkatensis 'Glauca', a 4 year old plant.

Chamaecyparis nootkatensis 'Compacta'

D. 75cm.–1m.   U.H. 3–4m.
Although a rather dull green colour, this globular slow growing bush is not unattractive. Its appearance is rather like a dwarf—but duller *C. lawsoniana* 'Pottenii'. Unlike the latter however, it is very tough and hardy and will not turn a hair in extreme weather conditions.

Chamaecyparis nootkatensis 'Glauca'

L. 2–2·5m.   U.H. 25–30m.
With the foliage colour of this cultivar being a deep sea green it is difficult to see how it came by the name 'Glauca' which means "Glaucous" or bluish. Like the species it will make a handsome tree where space is available.

Chamaecyparis nootkatensis 'Lutea'

L. 2–3m.   U.H. 25–30m.
There appear to be some different "clones" or forms of this cultivar in cultivation as some wide variations in the golden-yellow foliage can be seen.
At its best it is an attractive specimen, but does at any rate seem to lose the golden tones with age. This cultivar is also seen under the name 'Aurea'.

Chamaecyparis nootkatensis 'Pendula'

L. 2–3m.   U.H. 25–30m.
This is one of the most pendulous of the larger growing conifers, and although slow to build up shape and form it becomes a most distinct and handsome tree. Like all pendulous forms it needs the leading shoot training when young to assume a vertical position. This cultivar is similar to the species in that the foliage is dull green and coarse to the touch.

Chamaecyparis nootkatensis 'Lutea'.

Chamaecyparis nootkatensis 'Pendula'. – *A fine 10 year old specimen.*

Chamaecyparis obtusa

This species which becomes a large forest tree originates from Japan, and is known as the "Hinoki Cypress". The species is not grown much in Western Europe, but it has produced a great many good garden cultivars, many of them dwarf growing. Most of the cultivars have the short flattened sprays of the species and share its dark glossy green foliage with white x-like markings underneath. The "Hinoki Cypress" and some of its cultivars are often used in what one regards as a typical "Japanese Garden" and also for "Bonsai" culture, the artificial dwarfing and training of trees.

A scene from the heather garden at Bressingham Gardens. This is a five year old planting and already a complete ground cover has been achieved. This photograph was taken in June and whilst no heathers are yet in flower an effective form and colour pattern is evident. The plant in the foreground is *Thuja orientalis* 'Conspicua'.

Chamaecyparis obtusa 'Intermedia'

D. 15cm.   U.H. 30–40cm.

For the sake of simplicity I am intending to mention a few forms under this cultivar which appear to me and probably to the average gardener as being almost identical. Just before the First World War at Red Lodge Nursery, at that time near Southampton, several dwarf seedlings forms of *C. obtusa* 'Nana Gracilis' were discovered, selected and propagated. All were green, very compact growing cultivars, some much dwarfer than others. Most, though attractive, cannot now be considered good garden plants, tending to scorch in summer and burn in winter and are usually best grown in an alpine house. *C. obtusa* 'Intermedia' is about the smallest of the cultivars which could be considered for general garden usage and then only in miniature surroundings. It makes a dark green globular bush. Should any reader wish to obtain any of the other cultivars there are two fairly distinct forms in *C. o.* 'Juniperoides' and *C. o.* 'Caespitosa' which should be available from specialists.

Chamaecyparis obtusa 'Crippsii'

M. 2m.   U.H. 7–8m.

This cultivar is a rich golden-yellow with a rather open habit. It takes time and sometimes patience to train it into a good specimen, needing light pruning from time to time to achieve density. It has an excellent winter colour but requires a fairly open position to achieve its best. The frond-like sprays droop slightly at the tips creating a most graceful appearance. This is one of these trees that when well grown is superb but when placed wrongly can look very miserable!

Chamaecyparis obtusa 'Kosteri'

D. 30–45cm.   U.H. 1–1·25m.

The growth of this cultivar is very distinctive, the flattened sprays twisting both up and down. It has a bright green colour in summer bronzing in winter. It takes time to establish its character but eventually becomes a real gem of a plant.

Chamaecyparis obtusa 'Nana'

D. 15–20cm.   U.H. 50–60cm.

It will be already evident to readers that some confusion exists in the naming of some of the dwarf *Chamaecyparis obtusa* cultivars and this cultivar is no exception. It is often confused with 'Nana Gracilis' although 'Nana' is very much slower in growth, making tiers of cup shaped branchlets in the form of a flat topped miniature bush. It is an ideal plant for the rock garden, becoming wider than high with age, but certainly not likely to be an embarrassment to even the smallest of gardens!

Chamaecyparis obtusa 'Nana Gracilis'. – *A fine 15 year old specimen.*

Chamaecyparis obtusa 'Nana Aurea'

D. 30–45cm.   U.H. 1·50–2m.

This cultivar would appear to be one which has a golden-yellow colour turning to green in the plant and making a definite leader much after the style of 'Nana Gracilis'. Whilst a pleasing conifer it does not compare either in habit or in the brightness of 'Nana Lutea', which has more the habit of 'Nana'.

Chamaecyparis obtusa 'Nana Lutea'. – *A 5 year old plant in winter.*

Chamaecyparis obtusa 'Nana Gracilis'

D. 50–60cm.   U.H. 4–5m.

This is obviously much quicker growing than 'Nana', with much larger shell shaped sprays of dark glossy green, tending to make a more conical bush with age. It is the cultivar of *C. obtusa* that is most often seen in gardens and is deservedly popular.

Chamaecyparis obtusa 'Pygmaea'. – A young 4 year old plant.

Chamaecyparis obtusa 'Tetragona Aurea'.

Chamaecyparis obtusa 'Nana Lutea'

D. 20–30cm.   U.H. 75cm.–1m.

This cultivar is sometimes offered under the name 'Nana Aurea' but it is a much more attractive plant. As the photograph demonstrates it has a compact habit, somewhat similar to 'Nana' but slightly more open and a beautiful white and gold foliage. It seems to hold its colour throughout the winter and must in my opinion be considered one of the best of all dwarf conifers. Unfortunately it is still rather scarce in cultivation and will generally only be found in specialist catalogues.

Chamaecyparis obtusa 'Pygmaea'

D. S.P. 15–20cm. x S. 50–60cm.
U.H. 75cm.–1m. x U.S. 1–1·5m.

The flat fan shaped branchlets of this cultivar form a low spreading bush. The foliage is green turning to bronze-green in winter. Of similar habit is 'Pygmaea Aurescens' which has a much richer winter colour of copper bronze.

Chamaecyparis obtusa 'Tetragona Aurea'

M. 60–90cm.   U.H. 4–6m.

One cannot confuse this cultivar with any other! This is more on account of its colour and foliage however, as one does see this conifer in many different shapes and sizes. It has strong leading branches with no clearly defined single leader, covered with congested moss-like foliage. It needs full sun to obtain its best colour of rich golden-yellow. Plants grown in even a little shade turn a yellow green. Unpruned it will grow into an angular and uneven shaped shrub and therefore it is advisable to prune lightly to achieve density and a better form. This is a very attractive cultivar where grown well but the foliage does sometimes have a tendency to scorch in summer and windburn in winter.

Chamaecyparis pisifera
'Boulevard'. – *An
8 year old
specimen.*

Chamaecyparis pisifera
'Filifera Aurea'. –
*A 5 year old plant
photographed in
February.*

Chamaecyparis pisifera

Originating from Japan the "Sawara Cypress" has given us many valuable garden conifers, although the species itself cannot be considered so. Nearly all the cultivars share its liking for moist soils and humid conditions. They do not generally succeed so well in very dry conditions or on heavy clay soils, particularly those containing lime.

Chamaecyparis pisifera 'Boulevard'

D. 1–1·30m.   U.H. 3–4m.

An outstanding cultivar of fairly recent introduction, this has become one of the most popular conifers. Its silvery-blue foliage is especially intense during the summer months but it remains attractive all the year round. It will stand light trimming, which will help keep the foliage more dense and avoid the occasional open patch seen on some older specimens. Definitely this is a conifer to be recommended, though one should keep in mind that the same likes and dislikes apply as those given for the species.

Chamaecyparis pisifera 'Filifera'.
A mature specimen of graceful habit.

Chamaecyparis pisifera 'Filifera Aurea'

D.–M. 75cm.–1·25m.   U.H. 3–5m.

The 'Filifera' forms of the species are quite distinct, all having thin thread-like foliage. Young plants often look straggly, but with age they assume the typical broadly conical shape and become most attractive garden plants as the photographs show. 'Filifera' is the largest growing, followed by 'Filifera Aurea', which in an open position holds its bright yellow colour the year round. *C. p.* 'Filifera Nana' is similar in colour to 'Filifera' but is much slower in growth becoming a compact rounded bush.

Chamaecyparis pisifera 'Nana'

D. 10–15cm.   U.H. 50–60cm. x U.S. 1·5m.

This in its best form is one of the dwarfest of conifers—a tightly congested mass of dark green. There are other forms seen under this name which tend to be unstable and these should be called 'Compacta'. They are usually looser in growth and have the tendency to throw up a leading shoot from time to time. 'Nana' remains very dense and will eventually form a dome-shaped bush.

There is an attractive yellow-variegated form which has the same habit as 'Nana' called 'Nana Aureovariegata'. In a sunny position it has a lustrous golden appearance.

Chamaecyparis pisifera 'Nana'. – A 5 year old plant.

Chamaecyparis pisifera 'Plumosa Aurea Nana'. A 10 year old plant.

Chamaecyparis pisifera 'Plumosa Rogersii'. Some plants assume a more conical shape than this 10 year old specimen.

Chamaecyparis pisifera 'Plumosa Aurea'

M. 1–1·50m.   U.H. 5–7m.

The foliage sprays on the 'Plumosa' types are much softer and more feathery in appearance than the species, having what is referred to as "semi-juvenile foliage". This cultivar is slow growing with light golden foliage in summer turning to yellow-green in winter. All the 'Plumosa' cultivars will stand some trimming but dislike soils of heavy clay or high in lime.

Chamaecyparis pisifera 'Plumosa Aurea Nana'

D. 50–60cm. U.H. 1–1·5m.

A very compact form of 'Plumosa Aurea' this has the added value of keeping a much better colour throughout the winter, when it is extremely bright. There does appear to be more than one form of this cultivar in circulation, some not so good as the one I have described which is shown in the photograph.

Chamaecyparis pisifera 'Plumosa Rogersii'

D. 30–40cm.   U.H. 75cm.–1m.

This cultivar has foliage which more closely resembles the 'Squarrosa' types, which is more juvenile. It normally makes a conical bush, bright golden-yellow in summer, but losing this somewhat in winter. Also known as 'Aurea Rogersii' it tends to burn in cold drying winds and will benefit from being placed in a sheltered position.

Chamaecyparis pisifera 'Squarrosa Sulphurea'

D. 1·1–5m.   U.H. 3–4m.

Similar in habit to 'Squarrosa' this cultivar turns from light bluish-green to a bright sulphur in the summer months. It is at this time of course that it attracts the eye, as during the rest of the year it makes very little show, although its graceful feathery habit does add useful form to the garden.

Chamaecyparis pisifera 'Squarrosa Sulphurea'.
This plant is aged about 10 years.

Chamaecyparis thyoides 'Andelyensis'. – *A fine 15 year old plant.*

Chamaecyparis thyoides

This species known as the "White Cypress" is a medium to large sized tree originating from North America. It is found growing from Maine to Florida and does particularly well on swampy land.

Chamaecyparis thyoides 'Andelyensis'

D–M. 75cm.–1m.   U.H. 5–7m.

This is the cultivar of *C. thyoides* most widely grown in Western Europe and is an excellent garden plant. The branches are crowded with short leaves of bluish-green, turning slightly bronze in winter. Although eventually a medium sized tree it is very slow growing and not likely to cause embarrassment inside 20 or 30 years! It does not appear to thrive on lime soils and does better where moist than dry. It is also known under the name *C.* 'leptoclada'

Chamaecyparis thyoides 'Ericoides'

D. 45–60cm.   U.H. 1–1·5m.

A deep bronze-green in summer, this cultivar turns plum-purple in winter and is attractive mainly for that reason. It has close juvenile foliage which tends to burn in winter. 'Ericoides' is similar in looks and habit to one or two of the juvenile cultivars of *Thuja orientalis* and like them has the drawback of tenderness. Also like them it is often prone to be damaged by snow.

Cryptomeria japonica 'Elegans'. – *A fine specimen aged 15 years*

CRYPTOMERIA

Cryptomeria japonica is the only species in this genus, but it has given rise to a great many cultivars of garden value. C. japonica is native to Japan and China, and there becomes a large forest tree upwards of 40–50m. It has a broadly conical shape with bright green leaves closely adpressed to the branchlets. In winter the colour changes to bronze-green and this is also particularly pronounced with some of its cultivars. C. japonica is not much grown in Western Europe as a garden plant, becoming far too large for all but the most spacious situations. Both the species and its cultivars seem to thrive better in moist rather than dry soils.

Cryptomeria japonica 'Elegans'

M. 1·50–2m.   U.H. 6–8m.

This is a juvenile foliaged cultivar making a large bush or small tree. Browny-green in summer, the foliage turns a very attractive copper-bronze in autumn and winter. Although it will grow reasonably well in some shade it will keep a more compact habit if grown in a more open position and will not be so likely to be damaged by snow. It may be necessary to tie the tree after some years to prevent this happening.

Cryptomeria japonica 'Lobbii Nana'. – *A 5 year old plant in March against a background of Erica carnea* 'Carnea'.

Cryptomeria japonica 'Globosa Nana'

D. 30–50cm.   U.H. 2m.

Although slow to attain a definite form this dwarf cultivar has the typical foliage of the species but forms a neat rounded bush, wider than high. The branchlets are closely crowded and irregular, seeming to fall on top of each other. The colour is yellowish-green in summer, bluish in winter, and is not to be confused with the cultivar 'Globosa' which turns an unattractive rust-red in winter.

Cryptomeria japonica 'Lobbii Nana'

D. 50–60cm.   U.H. 2–2·5m.

An attractive and graceful looking plant, this cultivar makes a rounded bush, the foliage growth comes in bunches with new leaves shooting out like tentacles from the congested tips of the branches. Light green in summer it becomes a bronze-green in winter. This cultivar is sometimes wrongly seen under the label *C. j.* 'Elegans Compacta.'

Cryptomeria japonica 'Spiralis'.

Cryptomeria japonica 'Vilmoriniana'. – *A 15 year old specimen.*

Cryptomeria japonica 'Spiralis'

D. 40–60cm.   U.H. 1·5–2m.

This cultivar is distinctive in that the leaves twist round the stem of the branchlets, hence its name, but also for the fact that it stays quite a bright green the year round. It is very slow growing, forming one or two leading shoots, but otherwise becoming a somewhat irregular bush. There appears to be two distinct clones of this cultivar, one of tree-like proportions, but mostly those offered by nurserymen will be the one described here.

Cryptomeria japonica 'Vilmoriniana'

D. 25–30cm.   U.H. 1m.

A popular dwarf conifer, this makes a tight congested bush, particularly in open situations. It turns a rich red-purple in winter but the centre of the plant, because it is tightly packed, can get burnt when snow lingers and freezes. There is another cultivar very close to 'Vilmoriniana' called 'Compressa' which is even tighter in growth and more purple in winter. As is inevitable one sees these plants often grown and sold under the wrong label, but whichever plant one obtains it will be worth having!

Top right :
Part of the Pygmy Pinetum at Devizes,
Wiltshire, showing the natural
use of Dwarf Conifers.

Bottom right :
A view of Conifers and Heathers
in the Author's Garden at Bressingham.

Cupressus glabra 'Conica'. – *Better known as Cupressus arizonica* 'Conica'.

CUPRESSUS

Before the botanists separated the two genera the Chamaecyparis species were included under the genus Cupressus and are often still referred to by this name. The species of this genus are usually conical or columnar in habit, with tight rounded branchlets and leaves. The branching of the foliage is often irregular and twisted and the cones larger than the Chamaecyparis species. They usually make one central stem and underground a tap root which makes them difficult to transplant except from a pot. The taller species and cultivars are better planted when small and root pruning from time to time might help in establishing a sturdier root system. Staking will probably also be necessary to prevent the plant "listing" until well established. There are some good garden cultivars although some of them are not reliably hardy.

Cupressus glabra

M. 2–3m.   U.H. 15–20m.

To many it will seem most confusing to learn that when what has been known for years as *C. arizonica*—an attractive conical tree of blue-green—must now be called *C. glabra*; the true *C. arizonica* being green in colour although of similar habit. No doubt this change is due to the working of the 'priority' rule of the botanists, but one has to say that it is not always much help to the nurseryman, let alone the gardener, and the cultivars of *C. glabra* are likely in most catalogues to be named under the species *C. arizonica* for some time to come.

C. glabra 'Conica' and *C. glabra* 'Pyramidalis' as we must now call them are the two cultivars most normally in cultivation. Both are conical or pyramidal in outline with very attractive blue-grey foliage. It would confuse the issue still further to try to describe the small difference between these two cultivars.

Cupressus macrocarpa

L. 5–6m.   U.H. 20m.

The "Monterey Cypress" was much planted in England from the time of its introduction in 1839 until after the last World War. It has since been superseded by x *Cupressocyparis leylandii* which has a faster rate of growth and is much hardier. The very severe winter of 1962–3 damaged the reputation of *C. macrocarpa* as many were then killed outright. It is conical when young, losing its bottom branches and becoming broad-topped with age.

It is a bright green, dulling with age, and coming as it does from the California coast regions, is a useful plant for seaside areas. In my opinion it is not a particularly attractive conifer nor a good garden plant.

Cupressus macrocarpa 'Goldcrest'

M. 2·5–3·5m.   U.H. 7–10m.
This is about the best of the golden cultivars of *C. macrocarpa*. It seems to be quite hardy in most areas of England and is a bright golden-yellow, particularly in winter. It needs to be planted in full sun to obtain this colour and may well require staking or root pruning until firmly established. If *C. m.* 'Goldcrest' is the brightest gold it is closely followed by *C. m.* 'Donard's Gold', itself an improvement on the oldest cultivar *C. m.* 'Lutea', although this last has a well earned reputation for succeeding well in coastal areas.

Cupressus sempervirens 'Stricta'

L. 2·5–3m.   U.H. 20–25m.
This "Italian Cypress" of narrower columnar form is a selected clone of the species, which is more variable. Of dark green colour this cultivar is prone to winter damage as a young plant, and for this reason is not particularly satisfactory in colder parts of England.

Cupressus macrocarpa 'Goldcrest'. – *An 8 year old plant.*
x Cupressocyparis leylandii.
One of the best of all hedging plants.

x CUPRESSOCYPARIS leylandii

L. 10m.   U.H. 25–30m.
The "Leyland Cypress" is one of the most interesting and valuable introductions in recent years. It is a natural hybrid between *Cupressus macrocarpa* and *Chamaecyparis nootkatensis*, combining the rapid growth of the former with the hardiness and graceful habit of the latter. Although several clones originated in England around the turn of the last century it has not been propagated and grown widely until the last 10 years or so.
It is now probably the most widely used conifer for hedges and screening. For the latter purpose it is excellent, planted at 1·5m. spacing upwards. It will succeed as a hedge where there is sufficient room for it to reach

x Cupressocyparis leylandii. – A 5 year old plant.

2·5–3m. high and a corresponding width at the base, but for the normal low garden hedge it is too vigorous.

It is very adaptable both as to soil and climate conditions, succeeding well even in coastal areas. Small plants (under 1m. high) are preferable since these establish themselves and put out "anchor" roots quickly. Larger plants must be well staked and/or guyed for several years if they are to succeed.

Once established, the Leyland Cypress grows rapidly, increasing annually by sometimes as much as 1m. in height. It soon fills out to make a broad columnar shape, withstanding even hard pruning without damage.

As a hedge it should be planted at 1m. spacing, trimmed lightly at the sides until it fills out and stopped at the required height, which should not be less than 2·5–3m. There are several clones in cultivation, most of them too close to distinguish one from another except to the experienced eye. Some specialist nurseries may list more than one clone or cultivar, but generally they all lumped under the name of *Cupressocyparis leylandii.*

GINGKO

Gingko biloba. – A fine young specimen showing its beautiful autumn colour.

This genus does not in any way resemble the average picture that one has of a conifer, but it is in fact one of the oldest of all, its ancestors going back over 150 million years. It is deciduous, having fan-shaped leaves of pale green, turning a beautiful butter yellow in the autumn before falling. The only species representing the genus is G. biloba, which is perfectly hardy and of easy cultivation, although somewhat slow growing in its early years. It will eventually make a quite large tree of 20m. or more and is commonly referred to as the "Maidenhair Tree".

Top right :
Part of a scree rock garden at Longwood Gardens, Pennsylvania.

Bottom right :
Form and colour in the garden of Mr. R. Hawkins, Brent Eleigh, Suffolk.

A sloping bank in the entrance to Longwood Gardens, Pennsylvania, planted with Juniperus sargenti. and Juniperus horizontalis 'Bar Harbor'.

JUNIPERUS

The "Junipers" must be classed as one of the most useful and garden worthy group of conifers, varying as they do in habit and colour and in their wide tolerance of different soils and climatic conditions. Many species and cultivars are extremely hardy, standing exposed positions well and it is partly for this reason that they are grown so widely in the United States. Some of the prostrate and semi-prostrate forms are extremely useful for landscape work and ground cover and I believe that many of them are likely to become just as popular garden plants in England as the Chamaecyparis lawsoniana cultivars are at present. They have the added advantage of doing well on most soils, including those with a high chalk or lime content. They will stand drought better than most conifers, but will do better in sunny positions than in dry shade.

The Junipers often have both adult and juvenile

foliage on the same tree. The adult leaves are small and scale-like, the juvenile long, pointed and needle-like. They can often be in widely varying percentages, with a young plant bearing all juvenile foliage, changing to nearly all adult with age. On the other hand it may retain a considerable amount of juvenile foliage even when a mature specimen. This all helps to confuse recognition and may well be the reason that the botanists have had such difficulty in sorting out the nomenclature.

When I was first becoming interested in conifers I nearly wrote in high indignation to a reputable nursery to complain that they had sent me the wrong plant for J. chinensis 'Aurea'. The plant I had seen in a garden had nearly all adult foliage whilst the plant I received had all juvenile foliage and I could see no resemblance! That is the same plant that you see in the picture of J. chinensis 'Aurea'.

Juniperus chinensis 'Aurea'

M. 1m.   U.H. 5–8m.

This cultivar of "The Chinese Juniper" has the form of the species, but instead of its greyish colour it is of a bright gold, this brightness varying from the juvenile to the adult foliage. It needs a sunny position, although sometimes the juvenile foliage will tend to burn in early years. It is an extremely good garden conifer, holding its colour very well in winter. It sometimes takes a little time to make a leader and form its conical shape, but it is well worth the wait!

Juniperus chinensis 'Aurea'. – A 7 year old plant.
Juniperus chinensis 'Japonica'.

Juniperus chinensis 'Japonica'

D. 50–60cm.   U.H. 1·5–2m. x U.S. 2–2·5m.

This cultivar consisting of mainly juvenile foliage is one of the most prickly of all the Junipers. It is a light green bush, compact when young, but throwing out a few leading sprays with age. It is a good garden plant, a different colour and shape than most conifers and deserves to be more widely grown. There appear to be one or two other cultivars very similar to 'Japonica', some more compact in growth, but often these may only be "cultivariants". There is a cultivar 'Oblonga' similar in habit but a darker green.

74

Juniperus chinensis 'Kaizuka'

D. 1m.   U.H. 5–8m.

If one likes a plant of symmetrical outline—then this is not for you! "The Hollywood Juniper" seems to have a thing about not growing vertically and it is mainly for this reason that it has such character. Its colour is a bright rich green, of mainly adult foliage and it would make an excellent colour contrast to 'Aurea'. The outline of the plant is irregular both in its "leaning" and branching habit. The foliage is clustered at intervals along the branches to the twisted sprays at the ends. A fascinating plant which should be added to the list for wider recognition in Europe, having already established its popularity in the United States.

Juniperus chinensis 'Kaizuka'. *A 10 year old plant.*

Juniperus chinensis 'Pyramidalis'.

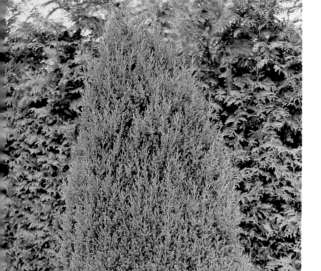

Juniperus chinensis 'Pyramidalis'

D.–M. 1·75–2m.   U.H. 3–4m.

This is one of the bluest of the Junipers and very useful as a garden plant with a similar rate of growth to *Chamaecyparis lawsoniana* 'Ellwoodii'. Plants grown in the nursery trade as *J. c.* 'Stricta' are almost identical with this cultivar, except that 'Pyramidalis' is very prickly to touch, whilst 'Stricta' is much softer. In both cases the foliage is wholly juvenile and the habit and growth rate similar. To keep the denseness in the foliage and to prevent getting brown patches it is advisable to give the plant an open position.

Juniperus communis

The "Common Juniper" has probably a wider distribution than any other conifer, spreading as it does from Japan through Asia, Europe and North America. It is generally seen in the wild as a medium sized tree or shrub of varying habit. It has produced some very useful cultivars for the garden, many of them prostrate and excellent for ground cover. As a rule they thrive best in sunny situations, growing particularly well on thin chalky soils.

The leaves are short and arranged in threes, being silver underneath and prickly to the touch. Some of these characteristics are accentuated in certain cultivars of the species.

Juniperus communis 'Compressa'

D. 30–46cm.   U.H. 75cm.–1m.

Making a tight conical bush this extremely diminutive cultivar is one of the best conifers for even the smallest rock garden. Specimens of 1m. are very rare indeed as 'Compressa' is not a particularly good "doer" and has a bad habit of being easily damaged by frost and wind. Nevertheless if one had to choose a selection of 10 dwarf conifers this would need to be in that collection. It is very effective planted in groups of 3 or more, particularly with the carpeting forms.

Juniperus communis 'Compressa'. – *These perfect specimens are 6 years old and only 40 cm high.*

Juniperus communis 'Depressa Aurea'. – *A group of several plants showing its wonderful summer colour and effective ground cover usage.*

Juniperus communis 'Depressa Aurea'

P.S. 1–1·5m.   U.S. 3–4m.

This is similar in form to *J. communis* var. *depressa*, the "Canadian Juniper", and like it, is an excellent cultivar for the garden. "Depressa Aurea" is a most decorative conifer, bronze in winter, the leaf tips opening up in early summer to a wonderful butter-yellow. The whole plant gradually becomes golden remaining so for most of the summer. The underside of the leaves is silvery-white and the plant is quite prickly. It needs a sunny position to grow and colour well, and plants grown in shade will give disappointing results.

Juniperus communis 'Hibernica'

M. 2m.   U.H. 4·5–6m.

With its fastigiate growth the "Irish Juniper" is probably the best known of the *J. communis* cultivars. It makes quite a narrow column in its best form, there being some clones more open in habit than others. A cultivar sometimes mistaken for 'Hibernica' is 'Suecica' the "Swedish Juniper" which is much broader and of a more open habit with drooping tips. The "Irish Juniper" is excellent for formal situations or in the heather garden, but has the tendency to open up with age, so may need tying.

Juniperus communis 'Repanda'

P.S. 1–1·5m.   U.S. 3–4m.

This cultivar is one of the best of the mat forming Junipers, growing vigorously and making a thick, dense carpet. The foliage colour is a dull green, bronzing slightly in winter, but planted as a ground cover in association with other colour forms such as *J. horizontalis* 'Glauca', *J. x media* 'Pfitzeriana Aurea' and *J. communis* 'Depressa Aurea' this cultivar can be most effective.

Juniperus communis 'Hibernica'. – *A 15 year old specimen.*

Juniperus communis 'Repanda'. – *One of the best ground cover Junipers.*

*Juniperus
davurica
'Expansa
Aureospicata'*

*Juniperus
conferta. – An
excellent ground
cover plant.*

Juniperus conferta

P.S. 2m.   U.S. 4–5m.

The "Shore Juniper" originates from coastal areas of Japan, and is a very useful and extremely vigorous plant. The photograph explains better than words how attractive this conifer can be hanging over a wall—it is equally adaptable for a bank or ground cover, needing a sunny position to look its best. It is a bright, refreshing apple green, particularly in summer—and very prickly to the touch.

Juniperus davurica 'Expansa Aureospicata'

P. 20–30cm. x S. 1m.
U.H. 75cm. x U.S. 2–2·5m.

This cultivar has mainly juvenile foliage with splashes of golden yellow all over the plant. There is only one non-variegated cultivar representing the species *J. davurica*, called *J. d.* 'Expansa'. This is quite a vigorous plant with rich green foliage, both adult and juvenile, growing in clusters along its branches, which are raised slightly above the ground. To succeed in growing this tough and hardy Juniper it should not be planted too deep. There is a further variegated cultivar which is similar in habit to 'Expansa' being more semi-prostrate than 'Expansa Aureospicata' called 'Expansa Variegata'. This has creamy-white variegated foliage.

Juniperus horizontalis

The common name "Creeping Juniper" aptly describes this species and its many cultivars as all are prostrate and ground covering in habit. Originating from North America where it is widely distributed, the species has produced a multitude of cultivars, unfortunately many indistinguishable from each other. They can all be considered excellent plants for ground cover, withstanding most extremes of temperature and succeeding on most soils. It would be hard to find a better subject for hanging over a wall or covering a bank. When using as a single specimen the habit can be most attractive, the plant push-out "whipcord" branches much like tentacles. Some cultivars will need more pruning than others to obtain density, and all will need some regular cutting back of the main growths to make the best use of them as ground cover plants.

The ultimate spread of some of these forms cannot be accurately given as most of them will root along the stem, thereby adding almost indefinitely to their diameter.

Although a great many cultivars are grown and available in the United States, the selection is more limited in England and on the Continent at present.

Juniperus horizontalis 'Bar Harbor'.

Juniperus horizontalis 'Bar Harbor'

P.S. 1·5–2·5m.   U.S. 4–5m.

A vigorous ground coverer, this cultivar has gracefully raised tips, bring the plant to 15cm. or so in height when established. It has thin branchlets, the leaves being a soft grey-blue in summer, turning mauve in winter. Like most of the *J. horizontalis* cultivars it prefers a sunny situation, tending to look scruffy where very shady. It perhaps should be mentioned that in the United States this name covers many clones and it is said there that there are as many different forms as there are nurserymen. So perhaps I am sticking my neck out in describing this very popular cultivar!

Juniperus horizontalis 'Glauca'. – *One of the best 'carpet' Junipers.*

Juniperus horizontalis 'Douglasii'

P.S. 1·5–2m.   U.S. 4–5m.

The 'Waukegan Juniper' like most of the *J. horizontalis* cultivars originates from the United States, and is used extensively there for ground cover. Although prostrate, the plant will throw up its branches to half a metre or so. These are covered with adult and juvenile foliage, grey-green in summer, purplish in autumn and winter.

Juniperus horizontalis 'Glauca'

P.S. 2–3m.   U.S. 4–5m.

This cultivar is a real ground hugging plant as can be seen from the photograph. The branchlets are numerous, whipcord-like in appearance, the foliage much thicker than on 'Bar Harbor' or 'Douglasii'. Although growing very close to the ground, the plant will build up with age, with fresh growth superimposing itself on the old. The colour is a steel-blue, particularly in summer. This is one of the best cultivars for ground cover and can even be used as a lawn!

Juniperus horizontalis 'Montana'

PS. 1·5–2m.   U.S. 3–4m.

An attractive cultivar with long slightly pro-cumbent branches of densely packed silver-blue foliage. It was introduced by Hillier and Sons, Winchester, and is claimed by them to be quite distinct and one of the best *J. horizontalis* cultivars.

Juniperus horizontalis 'Montana' *making excellent ground cover.*

Juniperus horizontalis 'Plumosa'.

Juniperus horizontalis 'Plumosa'

S.P. S.1–1·5m.   U.S. 2·5–3m.
The "Andorra Juniper" does not, as one might suppose, originate from Spain, but from Andorra Nurseries in Philadelphia, U.S.A. It is procumbent in habit to approximately half a metre in height, the branches growing upwards at a 45 degree angle, clothed in feathery grey-green leaves, turning a purple hue in winter.

Juniperus horizontalis 'Wiltonii'

P. 2–3m.   U.S. 4–5m.

To all intents and purposes this is practically identical to 'Glauca', perhaps being slightly flatter and slower in growth and more silver-blue in foliage than that cultivar.
It has been given some admirable descriptive names by the Americans such as the "Blue Rug Juniper" and the "Wilton Carpet Juniper" which have added to its popularity. We shall be seeing many more of these *J. horizontalis* cultivars planted in this country within the near future I feel sure.

Juniperus x media

This is the name now used by most, but not all authorities, to cover many garden forms previously listed under *J. chinensis* but in which the characteristics of *J. sabina* are more or less evident. The cross is said to occur naturally in N.E. Asia. Some controversy as to the desirability of the new name remains, so one is likely to find that there are books and catalogues still listing many forms included here under *J. chinensis*. The Media Group includes some very worthwhile garden conifers and could be divided in two main groups, the "Plumosa" and "Pfitzeriana". The former has mainly adult foliage, whilst the latter carries both juvenile and adult, and is slightly prickly to the touch.

Juniperus x media
'Blaauw'

D. 1–1·5m.   U.H. 3–4m.
The main growing branches turn outwards at the tips, away from the centre of the plant and contributing to its look of character. The leaves are scale-like and of a deep grey-green, the colour held throughout the year.

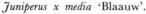

Juniperus x media 'Blaauw'.

Juniperus x media
'Hetzii'

M. S.P. 1–1·5m. x S. 2m.
U.H. 3m. x U.S. 4m.
This is a very vigorous cultivar and an extremely useful one. Used a great deal for landscaping and ground cover in the United States, this plant can be used to great advantage in many positions. Very hardy and tolerant of most soil conditions, even highly alkaline ones, 'Hetzii' can be used as a specimen plant, as a low hedge or as impenetrable ground cover. To improve density and appearance the plant should be pruned regularly. Keeping its grey-green appearance as it does throughout the winter, it must be considered one of the best all purpose conifers in cultivation. Be warned, however, that it is not really suitable for a very restricted space.

Juniperus x media
'Old Gold'

S.P. 1m. x S. 1·25m.
U.H. 2m. x U.S. 2·50m.
Of recent introduction, this cultivar promises to become extremely popular. It arose as a sport of *J. x media* 'Pfitzeriana Aurea' and differs from that cultivar in its more compact habit and in holding its golden colour better throughout the year. It is an excellent garden conifer and can be used in situations where 'Pfitzeriana Aurea' would become too large.

Juniperus x media
'Pfitzeriana'

M. S.P. 75cm.–1m. x S. 2–3m.
U.H. 2–3m. x U.S. 3–5m.
Popular and very vigorous the "Pfitzer Juniper" is used widely for landscaping purposes, but will become too large for the smaller garden. One sees old specimens varying considerably in habit, from prostrate to tree-like. It is very hardy and will do well in most soils and situations, succeed better than most Junipers in shade. The strong growing branches, consisting of mainly adult foliage, rise at an angle of approximately forty-five degrees, the tips attractively drooping. Like 'Hetzii' an excellent plant for many purposes, withstanding hard trimming well.

Juniperus x media
'Hetzii'.

Juniperus x med
'Old Gold'.

Juniperus x media
'Pfitzeriana'
*A 15 year old
specimen. Not to be
recommended for the
small garden!*

Juniperus x media 'Pfitzeriana Aurea'

M. S.P. 75cm.–1m. x S. 1·50–2m.
U.H. 1–1·5m. x U.S. 3–4m.

The "Golden Pfitzer" is of considerably slower growth than 'Pfitzeriana', the tips of the branches turning from yellow-green in winter to golden-yellow in early summer. A widely planted conifer 'Pfitzeriana Aurea' can add character to a garden with its irregular yet graceful habit. It can be effectively used as a single specimen or in a group planting, to accentuate a gateway entrance or a division of borders, to hide some unsightly corner or to mask a manhole cover. The cultivars 'Pfitzeriana' or 'Hetzii' have similar uses but variety can be introduced by the use of two, or even all three of these attractive Junipers.

Juniperus x media 'Plumosa Aurea'. – *A 12 year old plant.*

Juniperus x media 'Pfitzeriana Aurea'. – *This cultivar is most attractive when making new growth in early summer*

84

Juniperus procumbens 'Nana' *in winter.*

Juniperus recurva 'Embley Park'.

Juniperus x media 'Plumosa Aurea'

M. S.P. 75cm.–1m. x S.1m.
U.H. 3–4m. x U.S. 3–4m.
This cultivar bears mainly adult foliage of
the type with long, ascending branches,
gracefully arching over at all the growing
tips. The leaves are yellow-green in summer,
turning an attractive bronze-gold in winter.
Although slow growing for some years
'Plumosa Aurea' will eventually make quite
a large specimen. There are two variegated
forms 'Plumosa Albo-variegata' and 'Plumosa
Aureovariegata', the names of which are
self-descriptive.

Juniperus procumbens

P.S. 1·5–2m.
U.H. 30cm. x U.S. 5–6m.
Low growing and wide spreading this
vigorous Juniper raises its growing tips
upwards. It grows well in sunny well drained
conditions, blue-green in summer and a
purplish tint in winter. As a garden plant it
is certainly inferior to the following form.

Juniperus procumbens 'Nana'

P.S. 1·5–2m.   U.H. 15cm. x U.S. 3–4m.
This is a far more attractive form than the
species and differs quite considerably in habit.
Growing tight to the ground, it has bright
apple-green foliage, the tips of the branches
upraised with leaves shorter and denser than
procumbens. It is an excellent ground cover
plant for a bank, holding its colour throughout the year. The cultivar 'Bonin Isles' would
appear to be identical with this.

Juniperus recurva 'Embley Park'

P. 20cm. x S 75cm.
U.H. 30cm. x U.S. 2–3m.
This cultivar is at present not grown widely
but is a most distinctive garden plant which
should be better known. It makes a small
spreading shrub, with ascending branches,
but it is mainly of garden value because of
the rich green of its foliage, a colour which is
maintained the year round.

Juniperus sabina 'Blue Danube'.

Juniperus sabina 'Tamariscifolia'.
Used widely for landscape and ground cover purposes.

Juniperus sabina

Although this species has given us many good garden cultivars it is not of itself particularly attractive being very variable in habit. Usually seen as prostrate or semi-prostrate, the cultivars can all be distinguished by their pungent odour when the foliage is crushed. Both adult and juvenile foliage can generally be seen on most plants.

Juniperus sabina 'Arcadia'

S.P. 30cm. x S. 1m.
U.H. 50–60cm. x U.S. 2–3m.
Although classed here as semi-prostrate, this cultivar builds itself up by layers as do many other of the "Savin" Junipers. It has a similar habit to *J. s.* 'Tamariscifolia, although light green in colour. It is very popular in the United States as are two other cultivars raised at the same nursery of D. Hill and Co., Dundee, Illinois. The other two differ only slightly 'Skandia' being dark green and 'Broadmoor' a grey-green.

Juniperus sabina 'Blue Danube'

M. S.P. 1m. x S. 2m.
U.H. 1·5m. x U.S. 3–4m.
The name given to this cultivar is slightly misleading, for although an excellent ground cover plant it is by no means blue. The leaves are more of a grey-green and slightly glaucous underneath. A vigorous grower and high enough to smother weeds, it could well be more widely used for such purposes.

Juniperus sabina 'Tamariscifolia'

P. 20cm. x S. 1m.
U.H. 50cm. x U.S. 3–4m.
The most popular of the "Savin" Junipers, this variety makes a most attractive garden plant, building up height slowly with age, the branches overlapping each other. It is particularly good on a bank or a wall, the branches growing horizontally with densely packed juvenile foliage of grey-blue. There appears to be more than one clone in cultivation, some being more green than others.

Juniperus sargentii

S.P.30–40cm. x S. 1–1·5m.
U.H. 60–80cm. x U.S. 3–4m.
Widely grown in the United States for ground cover, the "Sargent Juniper" is an easy and reliable garden plant. The foliage is mainly adult, light green and densely packed. There are one or two cultivars of *J. sargentii*, such as 'Glauca' blue-green and slower growing, and 'Compacta' smaller and deeper green than the species.

Juniperus scopulorum

The "Rocky Mountain Juniper" is found growing in its natural state from British Columbia south to Texas and has produced many cultivars of garden value. Most of these are not yet known in England, but may in time well prove to be as useful and popular garden plants in this country as in the United States. There follows a brief description of some of these cultivars.

Juniperus scopulorum 'Blue Heaven'

M. 2m.   U.H. 5m.
A pyramidal form of neat habit, having very blue foliage the year round. It is also listed in some catalogues as 'Blue Haven'.

Juniperus scopulorum 'Gray Gleam'

M. 2–2·5m.   U.H. 5–6m.
This is an outstanding introduction in recent years and could be likened to a more dense and silvery *J. s.* 'Skyrocket'. Unlike many other *J. scopulorum* cultivars which become duller in winter, the silvery-grey colour of 'Gray Gleam' is accentuated. There is another cultivar of somewhat similar appearance in 'Hill's Silver' and 'Pathfinder' is also worth a mention with its broadly pyramidal shape and blue-grey foliage.

Juniperus sargentii. – A good ground cover plant.

Juniperus scopulorum 'Blue Heaven'

Juniperus scopulorum 'Skyrocket'. – *A 10 year old plant.*

Juniperus scopulorum 'Skyrocket'

M. 2–2·5m.   U.H. 6–7m.
Perhaps the narrowest, most "Pencil-like" of all columnar conifers, the name 'Skyrocket' aptly describes the habit of this popular cultivar. It has thin adult foliage of blue-grey and is quite a rapid grower. Some specimens seen are much narrower than others, particularly where planted in a sheltered or shady position. As the photograph shows it is an ideal accent plant, effective both as a single specimen or as a group.

A group of seven *Juniperus scopulorum* 'Skyrocket' at Fincham Manor, King's Lynn, Norfolk.

Juniperus scopulorum 'Springbank'

Juniperus scopulorum 'Springbank'

M. 1·5–2m.   U.H. 5–6m.
This cultivar has thin ascending branches somewhat open in habit with very distinctive silver-grey foliage, particularly in summer.

Juniperus scopulorum 'Table Top Blue'

S.P. 1m. x S. 2m.   U.H. 2m. x U.S. 5m.
Making a spreading shrub this cultivar has thin branches clothed with small silver-blue leaves. It will probably need some trimming to improve density.

89

Juniperus squamata

This species, though it is itself rarely offered, has given us a few interesting garden cultivars. Most forms are shrubby in habit with awl-shaped leaves and very similar in appearance to *J. procumbens* and *J. recurva*. *J. squamata* and its forms can be distinguished from these species by the tendency of the growing tips to "droop" or "nod" in a downward direction.

Juniperus squamata 'Blue Star'

D. 30–50cm. x S. 50cm.
U.H. 1m. x U.S. 1–1·5m.
The ultimate size of this cultivar cannot as yet be accurately estimated, although I have made a guess at it! Of very recent introduction 'Blue Star' makes a dense bush of steel-blue, the foliage and colour being very similar to 'Meyerii' from which it developed as a bud sport. It promises to become very popular.

Juniperus squamata 'Meyeri'

D.–M. 1·25–1·50m.   U.H. 3–5m.
This cultivar was introduced from China into the United States in 1914 and has since become very popular both there and in Western Europe.
It becomes a small tree or large bush in time, but is more attractive in its early years, for unless pruned back at regular intervals the dead foliage creates brown patches at the base. It will stand pruning well and in this manner will remain an attractive-looking bush. The foliage is a steel-blue and very dense, the branches ascending and irregular while the tips have the characteristic droop of the species.

Juniperus virginiana

The "Pencil Cedar" is similar in form and habit to *J. scopulorum*, being native to Eastern North America as *J. scopulorum* is to the Western region. Mostly forming a medium to large sized tree of conical habit, the species has produced a number of garden cultivars. The foliage is mainly adult and is often confused with *J. chinensis*, which has usually denser, more juvenile leaves. All forms are extremely hardy and adaptable to most soil conditions.

Juniperus squamata 'Blue Star'. – *A 6 year old plant.*

Juniperus squamata 'Meyeri'.

Juniperus virginiana 'Burkii'

M. 2–2·5m.   U.H. 4–5m.
One of the most attractive cultivars this has a compact dense habit with both juvenile and adult foliage, blue-grey in summer, purplish in winter.

Juniperus virginiana 'Grey Owl'

S.P. 30–40cm. x S. 2–2·5m.
U.H. 1–1·5m. x U.S. 4–5m.
A most attractive cultivar and useful ground cover plant this is supposed to be a hybrid between *J. virginiana* 'Glauca' and *J. x media* 'Pfitzeriana'. It has thin spreading branches, the leaves mainly adult and a distinct grey-blue. It is a good accent plant or can be used as ground cover in conjunction with other prostrate or semi-prostrate forms. Vigorous in habit it will improve density by occasionally pruning back the leading branches.

Juniperus virginiana 'Burkii' *in winter.*

Juniperus virginiana 'Grey Owl'. – *Effective as a contrast in form and colour.*

LARIX

*The "Larches" are one of the few genera of
deciduous conifers, fast growing and eventually
becoming large trees. They are not really suitable for
any but the largest garden or woodland, but in such
a setting they can add grace, beauty and character.
The leaves tend to grow along the branches in tufts,
somewhat similar to Cedrus and have the appearance of minute shaving brushes when first opening
in spring. At that time when bright green they
are most distinctive and attractive—and likewise in
the autumn when they turn golden-yellow before
falling. In winter the "twiggy" appearance of the
branches is accentuated by hoar frost or when
silhouetted against the setting sun. The Larches
are much planted as forest trees and will succeed on
most soils excepting those that are wet or chalky.
Although there are several species of Larch there is
only space in this book to mention two of the most
widely used.*

Larix decidua

L. 5–6m.   U.H. 25–35m.
The "European Larch" or "Common Larch"
grows rapidly, eventually making a large
tree, conical when young though not always
regular in shape. With age the tree usually
loses its bottom branches and those remaining
have a tendency to droop. The shoots are
light green, turning yellow in autumn, older
specimens producing green cones turning to
light brown. This species is a native of the
European Alps and the Carpathian Mountains, but is now widely distributed in cultivation particularly in forestry plantings.

Larix kaempferi

L. 5–6m.   U.H. 30m.
The "Japanese Larch" is another large
growing species and better known as *L. leptolepis*. It again is really too large a tree to be
described as garden plant, but there may be
situations in some larger gardens for which a
place for it could be found. The dormant
shoots are reddish and most attractive with
the winter sun on them. They turn a bright
fresh green in spring, turning yellow in
autumn. A very hardy species the "Japanese
Larch" is used extensively for forest planting.

Larix decidua 'Fastigiata'

*Larix kaempferi. – This specimen has been artificially
pruned to assume this uncharacteristic form.*

*An association
of shrubs and conifers
in the Dell Garden,
Bressingham.*

METASEQUOIA

This genus, dating from pre-historic times was thought to be extinct and was known only in fossils until a single living species was found, as recently as 1941, in an old Chinese temple. Since its discovery the "Dawn Redwood" described below, has been widely distributed and is to be found in many arboretums, parks and gardens throughout the world.

Metasequoia glyptostroboides.

Metasequoia glyptostroboides

L. 4–6m.   U.H. 30–35m.

This cumbersome name covers the only species known under the genus. It is a strong growing deciduous tree of conical habit, resembling *Taxodium distichum* but being narrower and more open in habit and with larger leaves. The branchlets carry flattened leaves, the appearance being feathery and plume-like. The colour of the foliage is bright green in early summer, becoming bronze, then golden in late summer.

The tree is quite hardy and grows rapidly doing best in moist but well drained soils. Where space can be allowed for its full development, it makes an attractive specimen and the fascinating story of how it came to light makes it a good "conversation piece" in any garden.

PICEA

One of the largest and most important genera of conifers, the "Spruces" have produced a multitude of good garden plants. The species are mostly conical in habit, particularly the larger growing kinds, but amongst the cultivars such is the variety available that almost any shape can be found! All of the species and many of the cultivars of the Spruces produce cones and these are oval or cylindrical in shape which, unlike those of the Abies, are pendulous in habit. The leaves are short and needlelike, the dormant buds often very conspicuous. Most species are varying shades of green, but some include cultivars which are blue, silver or grey adding considerably to the range of colour. They will succeed in most soils, but there are only one or two species that will do well in dry or impoverished conditions and not all will stand exposed positions. Some can be particularly susceptible to spring frosts, Red Spider and other pests.

Picea abies

L. 3–4m.   U.H. 30–40m.
The "Common Spruce" or "Norway Spruce" is the most widely grown *Picea* in cultivation and is familiar to all in Britain as the typical "Christmas Tree". In its typical form it is not a particularly good garden plant since although it looks attractive when young it frequently becomes somewhat unsightly with age, particularly if it has been dug up and used for several years to carry the Christmas decorations! It becomes a large tree, foliage dark green with brown winter buds and is used mainly for forestry purposes.

It occurs in its natural state in forests through Northern and Central Europe. It is sometimes still listed in some nursery catalogues as *P. excelsa*.

The dwarf forms have usually originated from a "Witches Broom", occurring on a normal tree, and since the stunted and sometimes malformed growth taken from one of these curious growths will strike readily from cuttings, the resulting plants have an attractive character of their own. But because of their origin these forms are liable to "revert"—throwing out strong and uncharacteristic growth. This should always be cut away as soon as it is noticed. There are a large number of these dwarf forms in cultivation and since some of them are very similar unfortunately much confusion and uncertainty exists in the nursery trade.

For a more detailed study on these dwarf forms than is possible here, I would refer readers to Mr. H. J. Welch's book "Dwarf Conifers—A Complete Guide," already referred to on page 4.

Picea abies 'Acrocona'

M. 2–2·5m.   U.H. 6–8m.
This cultivar is mainly interesting for its capacity to cone at an early age. This can be seen from the young plant in the picture, which within 5 years has formed many large cones at the tips of the branches. The tree itself makes a large bush, spreading if not trained in early years, with pendulous branches.

It was discovered in Sweden at the turn of the last century and although by no means a rare plant, it will not be found listed in many nursery catalogues.

Picea abies 'Acrocona'
showing its striking cones in early summer.

Picea abies 'Clanbrassiliana'
A 15 year old specimen.

Picea abies 'Clanbrassiliana'

D. 20–30cm.   U.H. 2m. x U.S. 3m.
Specimens of this cultivar would appear to be somewhat variable, although there are many masquerading under this name which bear no resemblance to the true plant. This makes a very slow growing globular bush, sometimes almost flat-topped when young, but developing into a round topped small tree in old age. It has a very dense branching system with large conical reddish-brown dormant buds which are very conspicuous in winter. The leaves are a dullish mid to light green, and vary noticeably in size on different shoots on the same plant.
A similar form, widely distributed as 'Clanbrassiliana' is an equally good garden plant, but it forms a denser plant with leaves that are consistently smaller all over the plant. In his book Mr. Welch suggests that this might be the 'Clanbrassiliana Elegans' described by Murray Hornibrook, but he now informs me that further research convinces him that even that name was a mistake and that the correct name of this small leaved form is 'Elegans'.

Picea abies 'Gregoryana'

D. 15–20cm.   U.H. 50–60cm. x U.S. 1·5m.
One of the most popular of the dwarf "Spruces" this is very similar to the much rarer form 'Echiniformis' and indeed the two are often confused. They both make dense cushion-shaped plants, wider than high and sometimes irregular in outline in old specimens. The tiny globose buds are a shining yellow-green, but not so conspicuous as 'Clanbrassiliana' ; the leaves on both cultivars are a dull grey-green, very narrow, rounded and needle-like.
'Gregoryana' differs from 'Echiniformis' in being more dense and having fewer, longer and very prickly leaves. For all but the enthusiast it shouldn't be necessary to obtain both cultivars.

Picea abies 'Nidiformis'

D. 30–40cm. x S. 45–60cm.
U.H. 1–2m. x U.S. 2–3m.
This is a distinct and excellent garden cultivar with a flat-topped, spreading habit. It is very popular on the Continent where it was first introduced and deserves to be more widely known in this country. The plant tends to build up in horizontal layers, becoming quite large in time. The colour is dark green and like most of the garden cultivars of the Norway Spruce it is extremely attractive in early summer, when the foliage tips are a bright fresh green with the new seasons growth.

Picea abies 'Ohlendorffii'

D. 30–45cm.   U.H. 1·5–2·5m.
Another introduction from the Continent, this cultivar was raised in Germany as long ago as 1845. It makes a broadly conical bush with a very dense habit, the branching system spreading outwards and upwards and the branchlets irregular in growth. The dormant buds are very prominent in winter being dark orange-brown, whilst the leaves are small and a light yellowish-green.

Picea abies 'Procumbens'

D. 20–30cm. x S. 2–3m.
U.H. 1m. x U.S. 3–4m.
Although classed as a dwarf conifer this is one of the most vigorous of the prostrate Norway Spruces and will eventually cover a large area. The leaves are a medium green colour, the branches layered, the branchlets having ascending tips.

Picea abies 'Gregoryana'. – This specimen is over 15 years old.

Picea abies 'Pumila'

D. 20–30cm. x S. 2–3m.
U.H. 1–1·5m. x U.S. 3–4m.
This form is somewhat uncommon in cultivation so *P. a.* 'Pumila Nigra' should perhaps be included in this description.
Both these cultivars make an irregular flat-topped bush with the lower branches semi-prostrate, the upper ones more erect. 'Pumila' makes a low spreading bush of bright green, but the form much more commonly found in the trade is a much darker green and dull in appearance. Both are reliably low growing forms where a less prostrate plant than 'Procumbens' is required.

Picea abies 'Nidiformis'. – One of the most popular dwarf spruces.

Picea abies 'Ohlendorffii'. –

Picea abies 'Reflexa'

Prostrate or M.
It is not possible to state an ultimate height and growth of this cultivar since left to its own devices it will become a sprawling prostrate plant several metres across. Trees of several metres in height are known but such specimens will have been trained up a stem when young. Such a tree with its pendulous main branches and all the growing tips sweeping upwards is most attractive, and the untrained or prostrate form is very effective planted on a large rock garden over which it can "cascade". It has prominent orange-brown buds, the foliage a dark blue or grey-green. Another pendulous form which makes a narrow column with its branches completely pendulous is *P. a.* 'Inversa'.

Picea breweriana.

Picea glauca 'Albertiana Conica'.
A winter shot of a very old specimen.

Picea glauca 'Albertiana Conica'.
An 8 year old plant making fresh spring growth.

Picea engelmannii.

Picea breweriana

L. 1–2m.   U.H. 15–20m.

One of the most beautiful of all conifers "Brewer's Weeping Spruce" is deservedly popular, although not always the easiest species to establish. Of broadly conical habit its branches are clothed with long pendulous branchlets, the leaves a dark blue-green. Like many pendulous forms it is not truly effective until several years old when the plant begins to fill out and take a more mature form. It will do well in both sun and shade but succeeds best in areas of high rainfall, originating as it does from the mountain regions of North West United States.

Picea engelmannii

M. 2–3m.   U.H. 20–25m.

This little known species is a most attractive garden cultivar with its broad conical habit and dense grey-blue foliage. It has conspicuous brown winter buds and bears reddish-green cones turning light brown on ripening which add further to its garden worthiness. It grows well in all except the driest areas. The selected form most often offered by nurserymen is *P. engelmannii* 'Glauca'.

Picea glauca 'Albertiana Conica'

D. 1m.   U.H. 2–3m.

This is one of the most popular of all conifers, being widely grown as a garden cultivar throughout Europe and North America. It first originated near Alberta in the Rocky Mountains of Canada in 1904, as a chance seedling from *Picea glauca albertiana*, the "Alberta White Spruce". If kept to a single leader when young it makes a perfect cone—forming a very slow growing miniature forest tree. Bright green in colour and dense in

habit, it becomes particularly attractive in early summer when the new season's growth appears. Unfortunately it is plagued by certain pests, particularly Red Spider mites and a few doses of a systemic insecticide may be necessary to control these in the summer months. This should certainly not deter anyone from buying this excellent cultivar.

Picea mariana 'Nana'

D. 7–10cm.   U.H. 30cm. x U.S. 50cm.

This very dwarf form of the "Black Spruce" is rather scarce in cultivation but is such an excellent rock garden plant that it should be included in this book. It forms a very tight, congested ball of grey-blue, with the blue predominant in summer. Very hardy and a real gem of a plant.

Picea mariana 'Nana'. – *This plant is 15 years old!*

Picea omorika in winter.

Picea omorika

L. 3–3·50m.   U.H. 20–25m.

The "Serbian Spruce" could be recommended as the best of the larger spruces for garden worthiness. It is both very attractive and adaptable to many soils and situations, hardy and not too rapid a grower. Forming a narrow cone, its branches are short and drooping and upward curving at the tips; the leaves dark green above, glaucous underneath; cones conical and bluish-black. It is very graceful of habit and deserves to be much more widely planted, succeeding well in highly alkaline soils and dry situations and not susceptible to pests as are so many other spruces. It is of course a forest tree in its original habitat in Yugoslavia, but can be effective both as a single specimen or planted in a group.

Picea omorika.
Like all spruces the cones hang downwards.

Picea orientalis.

Picea orientalis 'Aurea' making new growth in early summer.

Picea omorika 'Pendula'

M–L. 2–3m.   U.H. 15–20m.

This cultivar has similar foliage to the type, but is much narrower in form and its branches are, as the name suggests, much more drooping. An attractive garden tree which although slow to establish and in need of training in the early stages is nevertheless an extremely useful garden cultivar.

Picea orientalis

L. 3–4m.   U.H. 45–50m.

Perhaps, like a few other conifers mentioned in this book, the "Oriental Spruce" is eventually too large a tree for most gardens, but there is a place for it in certain situations. It makes a densely-branched, broadly conical tree, with the branches remaining clothed to the ground. The leaves are deep green, very short and overlapping, giving the branchlets a very neat appearance. The cones are purple when young, turning brown on ripening. It is a very distinct and attractive tree and adaptable to most soils and situations.

Picea orientalis 'Aurea'

M. 2–3m.   U.H. 7–10m.

Also known as *P. o.* 'Aureospicata', this is much slower growing than the species. It has creamy-yellow turning to golden tips in spring which are most attractive, as can be seen from the photograph, but these fade later in the summer to assume the same green as the remainder of the plant. Where grown well, and it needs an open position, it is a most effective cultivar.

Picea pungens

M–L. 2·5–3·5m.   U.H. 30–40m.

The "Colorado Spruce" is somewhat rare in cultivation as generally only the glaucous forms are grown and have become very popular garden plants.

Picea pungens glauca

M. 2–3m.   U.H. 18–25m.

There are considerable variations in habit, rate of growth and colour among the "Blue Spruces" and from any batch of seedlings one could select glaucous-blue forms that would make excellent garden plants. Many of these seedlings have been selected by nurserymen and propagated by cuttings or grafting, giving rise to numerous named cultivars, some of which are unfortunately almost identical. However such is the popularity of these selected Blue Spruces that they are often in short supply, particularly in England. Most forms have the typical rigid branching system, densely covered with stiff leaves of grey-blue. The winter buds are usually brown and the fresh early summer growth a bright eggshell blue, varying in intensity according to the clone.

P. pungens glauca and its cultivars are quite adaptable, very hardy and succeeding better in drier climates than some species.

All the following cultivars come under the "Glauca" group, and in many nursery catalogues "Glauca" precedes or is part of the cultivar name.

Picea pungens 'Endtz'

M. 2–2·5m.   U.H. 7–10m.

There have been and will continue to be arguments among gardeners and nurserymen as to which is the bluest of the Blue Spruces and I don't intend to enter into the arena on this subject! However this cultivar must be equal to any. It has a densely clothed, conical habit and is perhaps better known on the European continent than in England. There is another somewhat similar medium growing cultivar in *P. p.* 'Hoopsii' which is also claimed to be the bluest form in cultivation.

Picea pungens 'Endtz'.

Picea pungens 'Globosa'

D.45–60cm.
U.H. 1–1·25m. x U.S. 75cm.–1m.

This makes a slow growing dense blue bush, somewhat irregular in shape holding its colour well throughout the year.

Picea pungens 'Globosa'. — One of the slowest growing forms of the species.

Picea pungens 'Prostrata'.

Picea pungens 'Koster'

M. 2–3m.   U.H. 7–10m.

Perhaps the most popular and readily available, the "Koster Blue Spruce" has also been the longest in cultivation so perhaps has had an unfair advantage over its rivals! As mentioned earlier most of these cultivars will have been grafted and for the larger growing forms it may take at least two or three years of patient training to get the leader to go upright and for the rest of the plant to fill out. Usually it is well worth both the wait and the trouble.

P. p. 'Koster' is usually regularly shaped in form and silver-blue, holding its colour well in winter.

Picea pungens 'Prostrata'

P.S. 2–3m.   U.H. 1m. x U.S. 4–5m.

This is a very variable form, the name covering perhaps many cultivars in their prostrate forms. If a graft is made from a lateral branch as opposed to an upward leading one, unless trained upwards it will remain more or less prostrate. Often many prostrate or semi-prostrate forms will have arisen from the cultivars mentioned above and if a prostrate cultivar is required any tendency for a leader to develop should be stopped by a careful pruning of the offending branch.

These are really all cultivariants although one may find certain cultivars will produce more stable prostrate forms than others.

Picea pungens 'Moerheimii'. – A well shaped specimen aged 12 years.

Picea pungens 'Moerheimii'

M. 1·5–2m.   U.H. 7–10m.
This cultivar is another attractive and popular glaucous form, dense in habit and making a tiered effect with its layers of branches.

Picea pungens 'Montgomery'

D. 45–60cm.
U.H. 1–1·5m. x U.S. 75cm.–1m.
An introduction from the United States where it is very popular. It is somewhat similar to *P. p.* 'Globosa'.

*A view of the Rock Garden
at Longwood Gardens, Pennsylvania,
showing many mature specimens
of Dwarf Conifers.*

PINUS

The "Pines" form a large genus containing a great many species and cultivars some of which are of excellent garden value. Most of the larger growing species are conical or rounded in shape when young, becoming irregular and flat-topped with age. They add further dimensions of form and colour to the Conifer family, having needle-like foliage in bundles of two to five and quite unlike the leaves of most other genera. Cones vary in shape from narrowly conical to broad and rounded and many species retain these on the tree for several years although the seed usually ripens in their second year. On many species and cultivars the late spring or early summer growths are extremely attractive and often unusual. Also in late summer on many species the previous year's leaves drop leaving the inside of the plant unfurnished and so as they age many Pines assume a gnarled and rugged appearance, adding character to the landscape and garden. The photograph shown on this page illustrates this point admirably.

Among the Pines there are species suitable for most situations, many being quite content in poor dry soil where no other trees will grow, but one thing they have in common is a dislike for shady conditions and a polluted atmosphere.

Some species such as P. sylvestris and P. nigra are grown commercially for timber, but there are many slower growing species and cultivars suitable for the small garden and even the rock garden.

Pinus sylvestris.
The magnificient specimen in this picture is over 100 years old. Below it are trees aged about 20 years.

Pinus
aristata

D-M. 1·5–2m.   U.H. 3–5m.
The "Bristlecone Pine" is reputed to be the oldest living thing and although not grown widely in England or Western Europe it is quite popular in the United States. It originates in the South Western part of that country and old specimens have been found in some regions which are over 5,000 years old.

In cultivation it is often no more than a shrub with glaucous green leaves closely adpressed to the branchlets. It has the appearance of being covered in white resinous spots, which though unique may not be considered by some to be particularly attractive.

Pinus aristata. – The " Bristlecone Pine ".

Pinus ayacahuite, the "Mexican Pine".

Pinus
ayacahuite

L. 3–4m.   U.H. 20–30m.
The "Mexican White Pine" is a most graceful pine somewhat similar to *P. griffithii*. It is considered less hardy than that species, succeeding best in milder regions. The leaves are in fives, long and greyish-green. Long cones are borne on quite young trees.

Pinus densiflora
'Umbraculifera'. – *A 5 year old plant making new spring growth.*

Pinus griffithii.

Pinus cembra. – A 5 year old plant making new growth in spring.

Pinus cembra

D–M. 1–2m.   U.H. 10–15m.
The "Arolla Pine" or "Swiss Stone Pine" is one of the best medium sized garden Pines. Dense in habit it has the added advantage of remaining clothed to the ground with foliage even as a mature specimen. The young spring shoots are a distinctive orange-brown and it is by these that *P. cembra* can usually be identified from other five leaved species. The leaves outside are dark blue-green with a contrasting whitish-blue colour on the inside. The cones are erect, ovoid and dark blue. In my opinion this species should be better known and more widely planted than it appears to be at present.

Pinus contorta

M. 2–3m.   U.H. 5–6m.
The "Beach Pine" or "Shore Pine" makes a medium sized tree or often a large bush. It is not used much in the British Isles as a garden conifer, although as the common names suggest it can be a very useful tree for coastal areas, succeeding well on light sandy soils. It dislikes lime so should not be planted in chalky soils.
P. contorta is a two leaved species, the leaves being twisted and a yellowish-green, with the cones yellow-brown and usually borne in pairs or clusters.

Pinus densiflora

M- L 3–4m.   U.H. 25–30m.
The "Japanese Red Pine" is similar to the "Scots Pine", *P. sylvestris* in habit as well as in the reddish colour of its bark. The leaves are in pairs and bluish-green. Although conical when young like the Scots Pine, this species becomes irregularly flat-topped with age.

Pinus densiflora 'Umbraculifera'

D. 75cm.–1m.   U.H. 3m. x U.S. 3m.
The cultivar name 'Umbraculifera' is the latin word for Umbrella and this gives quite a reasonable description of the habit of this plant. It is slow growing, with densely arranged dark green leaves. It is a very attractive conifer and an ideal garden plant.

Pinus griffithii

L. 3–5m.   U.H. 30–50m.
This is one of the most beautiful of all the Pines, eventually making a large broad-headed tree and holding its lower branches in an open position. It originated in the lower Himalayas and is commonly known as the "Himalayan Pine" or "Bhutan Pine". Another five leaved species, the leaves being long and light bluish-green in colour. The cones are long, narrow and pendulous. Not every garden will have space for such a large growing tree, but certainly this species deserves to be more widely planted. Although tolerant of some lime it cannot be recommended for thin chalky soils. *P. griffithii* is likely to be listed in some catalogues as *P. excelsa* or *P. wallichiana*. According to some authorities the latter name is now considered to be the correct one but as *P. griffithii* is by far the most commonly used it seems sensible to avoid further confusion.

Pinus heldreichii 'Compact Gem'

D. 25–30cm.
U.H. 1·5–2m. x U.S. 1·5–2m.
This cultivar name has been given to a very attractive selected form of the "Bosnian Pine" *P. heldreichii leucodermis*. It is a dark almost black-green colour and dense in habit. Although it is not likely to be an easy plant to find in nurserymen's catalogues it will be well worth searching for. The "Bosnian Pine" itself is somewhat variable in habit, of slow to medium growth and making a very useful garden conifer. Like many other good plants it is not known nor planted widely enough.

Pinus heldreichii leucodermis.
An 8 year old plant of the "Bosnian Pine".

Pinus mugo

The "Mountain Pine" is so variable in rate of growth and habit that it is necessary to forego the use of symbols. Generally as seen in cultivation *P. mugo* is a medium to large shrub of dense bushy habit. It also goes under the name *P. mugo mughus* or *P. montana*. Being so variable from seed, selection has to be made to obtain the most desirable forms. This is how the named cultivars of this species have arisen, but they have after selection been propagated by grafting.

The young shoots are light green, the leaves are in pairs and dark green. *P. mugo* is a useful garden plant and adaptable to most soil conditions and being tolerant of lime. Only the dwarfer named cultivars can be recommended for the smaller garden as the species is likely to become too large.

Pinus mugo 'Gnom'

D. 60–75cm. x S. 60–75cm.
U.H. 1·5–2m. x U.S. 1·5–2m.
This is one of the most widely grown dwarf cultivars of the "Mountain Pine". It is dark green and of compact habit and very suitable for the rock garden.

Pinus mugo var. *pumilio*

D–P.
This is a botanical variety widely distributed in the Central European Alps. It is often seen as a prostrate shrub, spreading as much as 3m. and sometimes as high as 1·5–2m. It has an erect branching habit and very prominent winter buds, making it a most attractive garden plant.

Pinus mugo.

Pinus mugo
'Gnom'. – *One of*
the best Pines for
the rock garden.

Pinus mugo
var. *pumilio.* –
A selected compact
form.

111

Pinus nigra. — Sometimes better known as P. nigra austriaca, the "Austrian Pine ". This specimen is about 10 years old.

Pinus nigra

L. 3–4m.   U.H. 20–40m.

The "Austrian Pine" becomes a large tree although seedlings do differ quite considerably, giving rise to some denser, slower growing forms. It makes a most useful garden plant for the larger garden and is excellent for windbreaks. *P. nigra* withstands extreme conditions better than most Pines, succeeding well both on lime soils and in coastal areas. An all purpose plant indeed! It is an attractive species, usually of dense habit and dark green in colour. It is two leaved with young shoots a yellowish-brown, these making an effective contrast in spring. Conical when young it loses its bottom branches with age then becoming umbrella shaped. *P. nigra* is also referred to as *P. nigra austriaca* and as might be imagined originates from Austria and the surrounding regions of Italy, Greece and Yugoslavia.

Pinus nigra 'Hornibrookiana'

D. 50–60cm. x S. 60–75cm.
U.H. 1·5–2m. x U.S. 1·5–2m.
This form is worth mentioning as an attractive conifer for the small garden or rock garden. It is dark lustrous green, with a compact ascending branching habit. It was discovered as a "Witches Broom" on an Austrian Pine in Rochester, New York, U.S.A.

Pinus nigra maritima. – A young plant of the "Corsican Pine".
Pinus nigra 'Pygmaea'. A 6 year old plant.

Pinus nigra var. *maritima*

L. 4–5m.   U.H. 30–40m.
Often referred to as *P. laricio*, the "Corsican Pine" differs from the "Austrian Pine" in having a single, straighter stem with branches tending to be more horizontal. It is also of a more open habit with grey-green instead of dark green leaves. An adaptable plant the Corsican Pine is a useful timber tree and is grown widely for that purpose.

Pinus nigra 'Pygmaea'

D. 50–60cm.   U.H. 2–3m.
This cultivar was collected in the wild in the highest regions of Mt. Ansaro in Italy. It is very slow growing making a rounded bush, the leaves twisted and densely but evenly arranged. Normally a dark, dullish green it turns an unusual and attractive yellow in the winter months.

Pinus parviflora. – An 8 year old plant in early summer.

Pinus parviflora 'Glauca'. – This plant is 10 years old.

Pinus parviflora

M. 2–3m.   U.H. 7–10m.

Although in the wild the "Japanese White Pine" will make a medium to large tree it will very seldom reach its normal height in cultivation. A five-leaved species, with light bluish-green leaves which have silvery inner surfaces. The cones come in clusters or sometimes singly and are greenish-blue until ripe. Some Pines drop their previous years leaves annually but *P. parviflora* retains its leaves for four years so it is always seen densely clothed adding to its attraction as a garden plant. In my opinion this should much more widely planted than at present.

Pinus parviflora 'Glauca'

M. 2–3m.   U.H. 7–10m.

A selected clone of the species, this cultivar is a much better colour with a more ascending habit. When young it is rather sparsely branched and these tend to be somewhat irregularly placed. It is an excellent garden plant holding its bluish colour well throughout the winter.

Pinus ponderosa.

Pinus pinea. – A mature specimen in a garden setting.

Pinus
ponderosa

L. 4–5m.   U.H. 50–60m.

The "Ponderosa Pine" or the "Western Yellow Pine" is native to the Rocky Mountain areas of North America and although somewhat variable it usually becomes a large tree. It is narrowly conical in habit, the stout trunk having a reddish-brown scaly bark. The branching system is open, spreading or drooping whilst the leaves, produced in threes, are extremely long dark green and densely crowded on the branchlets. It is a most distinctive tree, but can only be recommended for the larger garden.

Pinus
pinea

M. 3–4m.   U.H. 10–20m.

Known as the "Umbrella Pine" or the "Italian Stone Pine" this is native to the Mediterranean regions and is not used greatly in more northern countries, being less reliably hardy. Its leaves are in pairs, long and light green, the habit rounded when young, becoming flat-topped or umbrella shaped with age. It does well in costal areas and is a common feature of Italian scenery.

Pinus pumila

It is extremely difficult to categorise this species through the use of symbols as it is somewhat variable in habit. Known as the "Dwarf Siberian Pine" in England and the "Japanese Stone Pine" in the United States, *P. pumila* usually forms a medium sized or prostrate shrub. It is closely related to *P. cembra* and some of the dwarf forms of that species are often difficult to distinguish from *P. pumila*. Of dense, usually mound-like form, the Dwarf Siberian Pine is light green with bluish inner surfaces to the leaves. There are one or two cultivars of this species which have been selected for their blue colour of which *P. p.* 'Dwarf Blue' is a most attractive form. The species itself is a most valuable garden plant, being extremely effective in the heather garden.

Pinus pumila. – An old specimen in winter.

Pinus strobus

L. 5–7m.   U.H. 30–50m.

The "Weymouth Pine" or "Eastern White Pine" is widely distributed throughout the Eastern part of North America. It makes very rapid growth and although looking not quite hardy it obviously is! Of pyramidal habit when young this becomes umbrella-like with age. Five leaved, the colour is bluish-green. An attractive tree in the young stages, *P. strobus* really becomes too large for most gardens, but it has given us a few useful dwarf forms.

Pinus strobus 'Nana'

D. 50–75cm. x 1m.
U.H. 2–2·5m. x U.S. 3m.

This name would appear to cover several very similar forms that have turned up in the seed beds. Plants offered under this name will be slow-growing, usually wider than high with densely set silver bluish-green leaves. As can be seen from the photograph it makes a most attractive plant.

Pinus strobus 'Nana'. – *A 6 year old plant in spring.*

Pinus sylvestris. – A young 5 year old plant.

Pinus sylvestris

L. 4–5m. U.H. 15–30m.

The "Scots Pine" is probably the most familiar of all the Pines to the British and with good reason—it is the only Pine native to the British Isles! It is somewhat variable in its rate of growth and habit as are so many of the *Pinus* species although usually the Scots Pine makes a medium sized tree, conical when young, becoming irregular and flat-topped with age. It has reddish bark, a notable characteristic, grey or blue-green leaves which are held in pairs. A common sight in the British landscape *P. sylvestris* is now planted even more widely for forestry purposes. It is quite adaptable to most soil and climatic conditions, but will not be so successful in wet acid or dry chalky soils. It has produced some useful garden cultivars, most of the dwarfer forms having been discovered as "Witches Brooms".

117

Pinus sylvestris 'Aurea'

M. 1–1·5m.   U.H. 5–6m.

This cultivar is much slower growing than the species and although a somewhat nondescript green in summer it turns a clear golden-yellow in winter and is then quite outstanding if carefully situated. It is particularly effective in the heather garden or against a dark background.

Pinus sylvestris 'Beuvronensis'

D. 60–75cm. x S. 1m.
U.H. 1–2m. x U.S. 2–3m.

This is the most popular dwarf Pine grown in the British Isles being often used as a rock garden plant. It is compact and densely branched in its best form, although as the photograph adjoining shows it may tend to become more vigorous and open with age. Several forms very similar to *P. s.* 'Beuvronensis' are in cultivation which can give rise to some confusion, but fortunately they can all be considered garden worthy plants.

Pinus sylvestris 'Aurea', *showing its golden winter colour.*

Pinus sylvestris 'Beuvronensis' *This 10 year old plant is beginning to lose its typical compact habit.*

Pinus sylvestris 'Watereri'. *A 6 year old plant.*

Pinus sylvestris 'Watereri'. – *This specimen is over 12 years old.*

Pinus sylvestris 'Watereri'

D.–M. 1–2m.   U.H. 5–7m.

A strong growing bush, conical when young becoming rounded with age, this cultivar is sometimes offered quite wrongly as *P. s.* 'Pumila'. It becomes quite large in time and is an attractive garden plant with its ascending branches and blue-green leaves. The original tree is still in existence in Surrey having been discovered in about 1865. It is now still thriving and has reached approximately 7·5m. in height.

119

PODOCARPUS

This is a large genus of evergreen trees and shrubs, but coming as they do from the warm temperate and tropical regions of the Southern Hemisphere, very few species are hardy even in the mildest parts of Great Britain. They are usually seen here as dwarf or slow growing shrubs, all having foliage somewhat similar to the Yews.

P. acutifolius originates from New Zealand and is reasonably hardy, making a dense medium sized bush with long pointed bronze-green leaves.

P. alpinus, native to S.E. Australia and Tasmania makes a sprawling prostrate carpet. To avoid the plant looking straggly the long shoots should be shortened to encourage density. The leaves are small and dark green.

P. nivalis, is in my opinion one of the most useful species of *Podocarpus* for temperate climates, making an attractive rock garden plant. It is one of the hardiest and most adaptable being quite tolerant of lime. It is very compact with small dark green leaves, although different forms in cultivation may differ somewhat in both habit and rate of growth.

A native of New Zealand where it is found in mountain regions it is known as the "Alpine Totara".

Podocarpus nivalis. – This tiny plant is more than 10 years old.

PSEUDOTSUGA

This is a small genus consisting of only five species. They are rather similar to the genus *Abies*, but have generally much smaller buds, similar in shape to the Common Beech and the cones are pendulous rather than erect. Most of the species dislike lime, succeeding best in moist but well drained soils.

Pseudotsuga menziesii

Pseudotsuga menziesii 'Fletcheri'. – *One of the most attractive of dwarf conifers.*

Pseudotsuga menziesii

L.5–6m.   U.H. 50–60m.

The "Douglas Fir" is a native of the Pacific North West region of North America and in its natural conditions makes an enormous tree. It has at different times gone under the botanical names *P. taxifolia*, *P. glauca* and *P. douglasii*. It is a fast growing tree, conical when young and becoming flat-topped with age. The leaves are small, soft to the touch and light green. In its typical form it is not a suitable conifer for the garden and it is primarily for timber that the tree is of such great value. Several slow growing forms however make excellent garden plants. It will not succeed in chalky soils.

Pseudotsuga menziesii 'Fletcheri'

D. 60–73cm. x S. 1m.
U.H. 1·5–2m. x U.S. 3 3·5m.

This cultivar arose from a selected seedling of the "Douglas Fir" and is one of the most attractive of dwarf conifers. It makes an irregular flat-topped bush with blue-green leaves which are soft to the touch. Among the dwarf conifers it is quite outstanding and should be more widely grown.

Two small Island beds of conifers and heathers in the Author's garden at Bressingham. All the plantings in this picture are less than 5 years old.

SCIADOPITYS

Sciadopitys verticillata

M. 1–1·5m.
U.H. 10–20m.

This unique and attractive tree is the only species in the genus. It is known as the "Japanese Umbrella Pine" and although not a Pine, its apparent similarity with that genus can be seen at a glance. It is extremely slow growing although eventually makes a medium sized tree.

The so-called "leaves" are similar in appearance to pine needles but arranged in whorls of up to twenty, and are a rich glossy green. The cones are also green turning to brown in their second year. Where grown well it makes an attractive garden plant, but it will not tolerate lime.

Sciadopitys verticillata.

SEQUOIA

There is only one species represented in this genus which is well known as the "Californian Redwood". This species S. sempervirens cannot in any way be considered a garden cultivar on account of its ultimate size, but no book on conifers could be written without it and besides it has given one or two interesting garden forms.

Sequoia sempervirens 'Adpressa'. – A 5 year old plant in summer.

Sequoia sempervirens. – A young plant which will improve its form with age.

Sequoia sempervirens

L. 5–7m. U.H. 70–100m.

The "Californian Redwood" has in its native area, the Pacific side of the Rocky Mountains, reached over 100m. but it is not likely to achieve that height in Great Britain. It was introduced in Britain in 1840 and the tallest tree is now measured at 40m. or so. It makes a stout trunk covered with spongy reddish-brown bark. The shape of the tree is pyramidal with drooping branches. The leaves are dark green above, whitish on the under surface. The Californian Redwood is often confused in peoples minds with *Sequoiadendron giganteum*, the "Mammoth Tree", or "Wellingtonia" as it used to be called, but the difference is quite evident from the photographs. Both are certainly too large for all but woodland areas or where large spaces are available.

Sequoia sempervirens 'Adpressa'

D–M. 1–2m. U.H. 5–10m.

This cultivar would appear to be botanically identical to *S. s.* 'Albospica' although the latter is usually looked upon as a medium sized tree. It is however, very slow growing for some years, and if any tendency to throw up strong leader growth is regularly checked it makes an attractive dense bush with its many growing tips of creamy-white. No damage will be done to the plant by hard pruning as *S. sempervirens* and its cultivars have the ability to break strongly from old wood. Treated thus *S. s.* 'Adpressa' is one of the most beautiful of dwarf conifers during the summer months, but if allowed to grow unchecked it will become a medium sized, somewhat untidy tree, often many stemmed and the particular attraction of the plant will be lost.

SEQUOIADENDRON

This genus again is only represented by one species S. giganteum, more commonly known in England as the "Wellingtonia". This also originates from California and is famous for its tremendous size and stature. It differs from Sequoia in its awl shaped leaves and larger cones, making a more symmetrical shape when young. The leaves are blue-green as against the browny-green of the Californian Redwood.

Sequoiadendron giganteum

L. 5–7m.   U.H. 70–80m.

The common names "Big Tree" or "Mammoth Tree" aptly describe's the largest living thing, for although it does not achieve the height of *S. sempervirens*, its girth is much greater. It beats the Californian Redwood for age also, being the older of the two at 3,200 years, almost 1,000 years older than that species. The tree when young is densely clothed, but with age the lower trunk becomes exposed. The bark is a very attractive reddish-brown and very spongy to the touch. It is seen quite widely planted in the British Isles in large gardens and country estates and is one of those plants that was very fashionable up until the First World War. One sees many specimens 20m. and over, but very few between the 5 and 10m. mark. Naturally it has slowly gone out of fashion and reflects the trend towards smaller gardens being definitely far too large for all but the most spacious areas. The "Mammoth Tree" does have a certain fascination on account of its size, but in my opinion it is also a most attractive architectural plant and could well be planted more these days for landscape purposes.

TAXODIUM

This genus is closely related to *Metasequoia* but originates from South Eastern United States and Mexico and not China. It is a small genus of deciduous trees with erect or spreading branches. The foliage is frond-like giving the trees a very graceful appearance. They are very adaptable, succeeding particularly well in damp swampy conditions, giving rise to its common name of "Swamp Cypress". However they are not happy where too much lime is present in the soil.

Taxodium distichum

L. 4–6m.   U.H. 30–50m.

The "Swamp Cypress" or, as it is called in the United States, the "Common Bald-cypress" is the form most often seen and makes a very beautiful tree. It makes a strong central trunk with reddish-brown bark, the branches spreading outwards and upwards. The leaves are bright fresh green turning bronze in autumn before falling. It has small rounded cones which are purple when young. Although probably the best conifer for wet conditions it will do well almost anywhere where not too dry. It is native to the swamps and riversides in Florida and surrounding states and there large specimens produce "Cypress Knees"—roots which protrude above the ground.

TAXUS

The "Yews" have been much maligned in the British Isles as garden plants in recent years, bringing to most peoples minds visions of old country gardens and churchyards! They are in fact among the most useful of garden conifers, being very hardy and adaptable to most conditions, thriving on chalk and tolerating a considerable amount of shade. The Yews are used to great effect in gardens and landscaping in the United States and it could be that we shall see a swing back to more popularity in Britain. There are a variety of shapes and sizes represented in the Taxus family including some very fine golden foliage forms. Some are excellent for hedging purposes withstanding clipping well. However, all species and cultivars do require good drainage.

Taxus baccata

The "Common Yew" or in America, the "English Yew" is one of Britain's three native conifers, along with *Pinus sylvestris* and *Juniperus communis* and makes a small tree or large bush. It is variable in shape and so no single symbol can be representative. It bears very small dark green leaves with red fruits.

Taxus baccata 'Adpressa Variegata'

D. 30–40cm.
U.H. 1·5–2m. x U.S. 1–1·5m.
This is a very slow growing cultivar with very deep golden young summer growths, the remainder of the leaves being yellow with a green stripe in the centre. As the summer progresses the leaves at the growing tips also begin to assume the green stripe. It is a most effective form holding a good winter colour. Quite often this form will be seen wrongly listed or labelled *T. b.* 'Adpressa Aurea'.

Taxus baccata 'Dovastonii Aurea'

S.P. 1m. x S. 1–2m.
U.H. 3–4m. x U.S. 3–4m.
A wide spreading bush or small tree this is the golden form of *T. b.* 'Dovastoniana' both cultivars having tiers of horizontal branches with pendulous branchlets. It often happens that this plant does not assume a leader and it then becomes similar to the photograph shown here, a bush wider than high. The leaves of 'Dovastonii Aurea' are yellow margined and cannot compare with the overall gold of *T. b.* 'Semperaurea'.

Taxus baccata 'Elegantissima'

D. 1m.   U.H. 3–5m.
Slow growing and compact with ascending branches this is a popular cultivar in Britain. It has yellow leaves when young, occasionally whitish and later the margins only being yellow.

Hedge of Taxus baccata.

Taxus baccata. – A 9 year old plant.

Taxus baccata 'Dovastonii Aurea'. – *A 10 year old plant.*

Taxus baccata 'Fastigiata'. – *A 10 year old specimen of the "Irish Yew".*

Taxus baccata 'Fastigiata Aurea'

M. 1·5–2m.   U.H. 4–5m.
The golden form of the Irish Yew is a much more attractive plant for the garden. It is of similar habit and rate of growth to that cultivar, but has deep yellow-green leaves, the yellow being predominant during the period of new growth in early summer. The winter colour is a striking old gold when planted in a sunny position. There is a slightly more golden and slower growing form *T. b.* 'Standishii' which could almost be considered a dwarf cultivar.

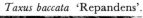

Taxus baccata 'Repandens'

P.S. 1–1·5m.   U.H. 50cm. x U.S. 3–4m.
This is a low growing, wide spreading form and very useful for ground cover purposes. It will tolerate dry shade or full sun so is extremely adaptable. It has long prostrate branches, with branchlets drooping at the tips, and leaves a dark shining green. There is another form *T. b.* 'Repens Aurea' which is golden variegated turning to cream and likely to become popular when better known.

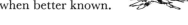

Taxus baccata 'Fastigiata Aurea'.

Taxus baccata 'Repandens'.

Taxus baccata 'Semperaurea'

D–M. 75cm.–1m. x S. 1m.
U.H. 1·5–3m. x U.S. 2–3m.

The American common name "Evergold
English Yew" aptly describes this excellent
garden plant. It is undoubtedly the most
golden of the yews making a wide spreading
bush with several semi-erect leading shoots.
It is particularly golden when new shoots
appear in late spring and colour is maintained
well throughout the year.

Taxus baccata 'Semperaurea' *making new growth in
summer.*

Taxus cuspidata 'Nana'. – *The leading shoots may
need pruning occasionally.*

Taxus cuspidata

The "Japanese Yew" is not used much in the
British Isles, but both the type and its forms
are widely planted in America. It is normally
shrubby in cultivation although in its native
habitat it is a small to medium sized tree.
The leaves can be distinguished from those
of the English Yew by the yellow-green under
surface. It is much hardier than the English
Yew, this being the prime cause of its wider
use in the United States. There, a great many
cultivars have been introduced which are
very similar, and it is perhaps worth mentioning one or two of the most widely used
forms.

T. c. 'Capitata', the "Upright Japanese Yew"
as grown in the trade in the United States is
a medium sized conical tree, used much as an
accent plant.

T.c. 'Densa' is usually listed in American
catalogues as 'Densiformis' or the "Cushion
Japanese Yew". It is a compact dwarf shrub,
broader than high with dark green leaves.

T. c. 'Nana'. This cultivar is one of the most
widely planted in Europe, having very dark
leaves, slow growing and compact when
young, but developing with age an irregular
branching system. If not pruned from time
to time it can become an untidy bush. The
cultivar 'Intermedia' would appear to be
similar to this.

Taxus x media 'Hicksii'.

Taxus x media

The "Anglo-Japanese Yew" is a hybrid between *T. baccata* and *T. cuspidata* and was raised in the Hunnewell Pinetum, Wellesley, Massachusetts, U.S.A. around the turn of the last century. As could be expected its habit is more or less intermediate between its parents, forming a medium to large sized spreading shrub. There are several forms in cultivation in the United States where they are very popular being vigorous, hardy and adaptable.

T. x. m. 'Brownii' is a very popular form in the United States making a compact column, as wide as it is high. The branches are semi-erect, branchlets densely packed and the leaves crowded and dark green.

T. x. m. 'Hatfieldii' is an excellent cultivar for a hedge, making a dense bush of dark green. It is of medium growth with sharply ascending branches, becoming pyramidal with age.

T. x. m. 'Hicksii' is similar in form to 'Hatfieldii' but more open in habit, and is also a suitable hedge plant. It is for this purpose that they may become more widely used in the British Isles.

All *Taxus* take well to trimming or shearing and it is the habit of many nurserymen in the United States to improve their saleable appearance by constant shearing. They make a far more attractive plant when treated this way though not always being exactly true to habit!

THUJA

This genus although being only a small one has produced many fine garden plants. In many ways they are similar to the Chamaecyparis, forming shrubs or trees of mainly conical habit and reproducing freely from seed. The tendency for many clones of similar appearance to get into general cultivation has produced similar problems to the Chamaecyparis. Three species of Thuja; occidentalis, orientalis and plicata have given us useful garden forms. They all have certain characteristics in common, flattened branchlets and scale-like overlapping leaves. One or two species have distinctly aromatic or pungent foliage, the choice of words to describe this is usually dependent upon individual tastes!

The Thujas are adaptable to most soils, but are usually less happy in swampy or badly drained situations. Thuja orientalis is the only species which could not be considered completely hardy in the coldest climates. Although hardy in Great Britain it will not normally survive Scandinavian winters nor below Zone 6 in the United States. Two species, occidentalis and plicata make excellent hedges. The considerable variety of sizes and colours represented make the Thujas an invaluable genus for inclusion in any garden.

Thuja occidentalis 'Holmstrup'. – *A 10 year old specimen.*

Mr. Welch describes it as an "unpleasant acrid smell" so it must obviously be a matter of personal taste! This species is the hardiest of the Thujas and is often used for hedging where *T. plicata* would not be sufficiently hardy, the latter undoubtedly making the better hedge. It has produced a great number of large, slow growing and dwarf cultivars.

Thuja occidentalis

The "White Cedar" or "American Arborvitae" originates from the Eastern United States, from Nova Scotia in the north, to Tennessee in the south. It is somewhat variable in the wild, but usually columnar in habit, reaching a maximum of 20m. or so. The branches are spreading, the branchlets flattened and spray-like. The leaves have conspicuous resin glands, are dark green on the upper surface, pale green underneath and turning bronze in winter. To my mind it has a pleasant odour when crushed, although

Thuja occidentalis 'Hetz Midget'

D. 25–30cm. U.H. 50–60cm. x U.S. 60–75cm. This is an American introduction and promises to be quite a popular little plant for the rock or miniature garden. It is dark green and probably the slowest growing of all Thujas. There is a dwarf globular cultivar introduced recently from Denmark, called *T. o.* 'Danica', which promises to become quite popular.

Thuja occidentalis 'Lutea Nana'. – *A 5 year old plant in summer.*

Thuja occidentalis 'Wareana Lutescens'. — *The foliage turns a pleasing creamy shade in winter.*

Thuja occidentalis 'Holmstrup'

D. 1–1·5m.   U.H. 3–4m.

Also known as *T. o.* 'Holmstrupensis' this cultivar deserves to be better known. It makes a neat conical bush with tightly packed rich green foliage maintained well through most of the year. It will in hard winters become slightly bronze tinged.

Thuja occidentalis 'Lutea Nana'

D–M. 1–1·5m.   U.H. 3–4m.

Although much slower growing than the form 'Lutea' this does not appear as though it will remain dwarf for long. It is an excellent cultivar, being almost more golden-yellow in winter than in summer. It has been com-

pared to 'Rheingold', but differs in being much more erect in habit with no juvenile foliage and much more yellow in colour. It should certainly in time become a very popular plant.

Thuja occidentalis 'Wareana Lutescens'

D–M. 1–2m.   U.H. 4–5m.

This is an excellent cultivar which is likely to become popular when better known, even though it has had every opportunity, being first introduced as long ago as 1884! It is slow growing, eventually making a small to medium sized conical tree. The foliage is compact with flattened sprays, the colour a light white-yellow green in summer, turning an attractive cream inside the plant during the winter. The delicate shades of colour are quite distinctive. It is also listed under the name *T. o.* 'Wareana Lutescens'.

133

Thuja occidentalis 'Pyramidalis'

M. 1·5–2·5m.   U.H. 4–5m.

This cultivar makes a useful formal tree, being mid-green and narrowly pyramidal in outline. There is a form grown widely in the United States, *T. o.* 'Nigra' which is broader based and deep green, the colour being maintained throughout the year. Both these cultivars are excellent for hedges and tolerate all conditions, from full sun to quite heavy shade.

Thuja occidentalis 'Recurva Nana'

D. 25–30cm.
U.H. 60–70cm. x U.S. 1m.

A useful plant for the rock garden, making a low growing flat-topped dome with erect and spreading branches. The branchlets are curiously recurved or half-turned at the end of the branches. It is light green in summer, bronze in winter.

Thuja occidentalis 'Rheingold'

D. 1–1·5m.   U.H. 3–4m.

Two forms are given for this popular plant because of its irregularity at different stages of growth. Many forms which have been propagated from juvenile foliage, normally taken from the base of the plant, make compact, rounded bushes, whilst those that have been taken from the upper part make a more open, conical form. The globose juvenile form will in time attain adult foliage and so become more conical in shape and resembling the typical plant shown in the photograph. The photograph shows the different types of foliage quite clearly. Whatever its shape 'Rheingold' is one of the best of all garden conifers, old gold in summer and turning a rich copper-gold in winter. It is very effective in the heather garden, contrasting with the winter flowering heaths. Some authorities claim there is a distinct form in *T. o.* 'Ellwangeriana Aurea', but I have never been able to discern any difference.

Thuja occidentalis 'Pyramidalis'. – *An excellent plant for hedges.*

Thuja occidentalis 'Rheingold'. – *A 8 year old plant.*

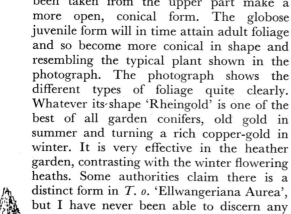

Thuja occidentalis 'Smaragd'

M. 2–2·5m.   U.H. 4–7m.

This cultivar was raised in Denmark which explains the cumbersome name. It is known in France as *T. o.* 'Emeraude' which is at least more pronounceable to the English tongue! It has a neat pyramidal habit, is a good plant for hedging and has the additional advantage of holding its bright green colour throughout the winter.

Thuja occidentalis 'Woodwardii'

D. 50–60cm
U.H. 1·5–2m. x U.S. 2–3m.

A strong growing cultivar of rich dark green, this makes a dense globular bush with rather coarse open foliage, arranged in a vertical plane. It maintains its globular shape without trimming and is particularly useful in certain regions because of its extreme hardiness and because it holds its colour well throughout the year.

Thuja occidentalis 'Smaragd'.

Thuja occidentalis 'Woodwardii'.

Thuja orientalis

The "Chinese Arbor-vitae" was at one time considered a distinct genus and the generic name *Biota* is still referred to in some books and nursery catalogues. It is normally a large rounded shrub or small conical tree to about 10m. The branches and branchlets are erect, with flattened sprays bearing small green leaves. These leaves are the same colour both sides of the spray and the species can be distinguished further by being less aromatic than the other Thujas and by its recurved cone scales. It has given us some extremely attractive garden forms, although some are of doubtful hardiness.

Thuja orientalis 'Conspicua'. – A 6 year old plant in early summer.

Thuja orientalis 'Elegantissima'.

Thuja orientalis 'Aurea Nana'. – This fine specimen is over 10 years old.

Thuja orientalis 'Aurea Nana'

D. 60–70cm. U.H. 1·5–2·5m.

The form normally grown under this name makes a globose, densely foliaged plant, golden-yellow in summer, yellow or bronze-green in winter. It has erect, flattened foliage sprays arranged vertically giving the plant a very compact, neat appearance. It is widely known in the United States as *T. o.* 'Berckmannii' or "Berckman's Golden Biota", but this name was originally given to *T. o.* 'Conspicua' described below. Because there have been a great many golden seedlings of *Thuja orientalis* raised and introduced into the trade some confusion is inevitable, but the plant shown and described here is generally accepted as the correct 'Aurea Nana'. It is one of the best of all conifers and would certainly have to be included in the British top ten!

Thuja orientalis 'Conspicua'

M. 2m. U.H. 4–5m.

This cultivar compares more than favourably with the more popular golden *Chamaecyparis lawsoniana* cultivars. It is of medium growth with golden-yellow foliage maintained better than any other *orientalis* form. This was raised in the United States by Mr. P. J. Berckmans and should logically bear his name rather than the form 'Aurea Nana'. It should become more popular in England when better known.

Thuja orientalis 'Elegantissima'

M. 1·5–2m. U.H. 4–5m.

This is another golden form, differing from 'Conspicua' in being somewhat slower in growth, with much more compact foliage which turns from old gold in summer to an attractive bronze in winter. All three of the golden cultivars mentioned are worthy of inclusion in any garden.

Thuja orientalis 'Juniperoides'

D. 45–60cm. U.H. 1m.

Also known as *T. o.* 'Decussata' this is one of the juvenile forms of the species and like all of these types it makes a rounded bush, never more than 1m. in height. It has dense foliage, greyish-green in summer turning to a rich purple in winter. Unfortunately these forms tend to open up with age and are easily damaged by snow. They are the least hardy of the Thujas and a reasonably sheltered spot should be found for best results.

Thuja orientalis 'Rosedalis'

D. 40–50cm. U.H. 75cm.–1m.

Probably the most popular of the juvenile foliage forms, it is distinctive in that it changes colour three times a year. In winter it is purple-brown turning in spring to bright butter-yellow then to light green in summer. The foliage is very soft and this together with its colour change distinguish it from another juvenile form 'Meldensis'. 'Rosedalis' is sometimes referred to as 'Rosedalis Compacta'.

Thuja orientalis 'Rosedalis'.
A 5 year old plant in summer.

Thuja plicata

L. 5–7m.　U.H. 30–60m.
The "Western Red Cedar" is one of the most
important timber trees in North America,
but it is also of great ornamental value being
used widely for screens and hedges. It was
introduced to the British Isles by William
Lobb in 1853 and is often still incorrectly
referred to as *T. lobbii*.
It is a fast growing pyramidal tree with
cinnamon red or brown shredding bark. The
leaves are a mid shining green above with
whitish markings beneath, borne on large
flattened sprays. The foliage has a very
pleasant odour when crushed. It is an
adaptable species and although happier in
moist soils, it will tolerate highly alkaline and
dry conditions. It makes an excellent hedging
plant, withstanding clipping well and it has

the added advantage of branching into new
growth from old wood. There have been
many good garden cultivars arise from this
species.

Thuja plicata 'Atrovirens'. – *One of the most attractive conifers for hedging.*

Thuja plicata. – *A specimen aged 10 years.*

Thuja plicata 'Atrovirens'

L. 5–7m.　U.H. 30–60m.
This selected form of the species differs in its
dark glossy green leaves and its more conical

habit. It is an excellent plant for hedges,
being more consistent in form and colour than
the species.

Thuja plicata 'Rogersii'

D. 25–30cm.　U.H. 1m.
This is in my opinion one of the best dwarf
conifers on account of its neat compact habit
and excellent colour held the year round.
The inside of the bush is dark green whilst
the outside tips are golden-bronze. It is

normally globular in shape, but throws the
occasional strong leading shoot which sometimes gives it a more conical habit.

Thuja plicata 'Rogersii'. – This specimen is over 15 years old.

Thuja plicata 'Stoneham Gold'; A 5 year old plant.

Thuja plicata 'Zebrina'.

Thuja plicata 'Stoneham Gold'

D. 50–75cm.   U.H. 2m.
This is as yet little known, but promises to be one of the best golden dwarf conifers in cultivation. It makes at first an irregular shaped plant, but eventually becomes erect or broadly conical. The inside of the plant is almost black-green and the outside a wonderful orange-yellow tinged bronze at the tips. The two-toned effect is very striking and as the colour is well maintained throughout the winter this cultivar is of great garden value and likely to become very popular.

Thuja plicata 'Zebrina'

L. 3–4m.   U.H. 15–20m.
Slower growing than the species, this makes a very attractive conifer with its light green foliage striped with greeny-yellow. In early summer it is particularly attractive with the whole plant giving a golden appearance and the green less evident. It will eventually become a large tree, so space should be allowed for its development.

THUJOPSIS
Thujopsis dolobrata

M. 2–3m.   U.H. 10–20m.

The genus *Thujopsis* is closely related to *Thuja* with *T. dolobrata* being the only species represented although it has produced a few cultivars. It makes a small to medium sized tree in cultivation although in its natural state in Japan it reaches 35m. Much slower growing than *T. plicata*, the species it most closely resembles, it also differs in its larger leaves and broader more flattened branchlets. It makes a broad based pyramid, the leaves dark green above, conspicuously silver-white beneath. There is an attractive golden form 'Aurea' which deserves to be better known and a dwarf form 'Nana' which forms a spreading flat-topped bush.

Thujopsis dolobrata.

TSUGA

The "Hemlocks" are a genus of ten species, being mostly medium to large sized, broadly conical trees. Their foliage resembles the yews, but is usually much thinner and arching at the tips giving them an elegant and graceful appearance. The Tsugas thrive in moist, well drained soils and will tolerate shady conditions. Some make excellent ornamental trees, particularly for the larger garden and one species T. canadensis has given us a great many cultivars, many of them dwarf forms.

Tsuga canadensis

Tsuga canadensis 'Bennett'. – One of the most attractive dwarf Tsugas.

M. 4–5m.   U.H. 30m.

The "Eastern Hemlock" makes a pyramidal tree and is the best species for alkaline soils. It has narrow leaves of light green with two whitish bands beneath. The cones are small, oval in shape and pendulous. The branching system is usually forked near the base which partly distinguishes it from the closely related species *T. heterophylla*.

The species originates from Eastern North America and it is from the United States that so many forms have been introduced into cultivation. Many of these are not yet known in Western Europe, but seem likely to become more popular when they are more readily available. There is at least one specialist nursery in England which offers a wide selection. Some are rather similar in habit, particularly in the young stages, and here only brief mention can be made of some most popular and distinct forms.

Tsuga canadensis.

Tsuga canadensis 'Bennett'

D. S.P. 30cm. x S. 60–75cm.
U.H. 1m. x U.S. 2–3m.
This is an attractive semi-prostrate bush of light to mid-green. The habit is compact and flat-topped with the branchlets drooping at the tips. It is also listed in some catalogues as 'Bennett's Minima'. The graceful and distinct form of this cultivar add further dimension to the range of garden conifers. There is a form 'Fantana' which is similar in habit but not so reliably dwarf.
T. c. 'Albospica' is slower growing and more compact than the species with creamy-white tipped foliage, particularly attractive in spring and summer.
T. c. 'Cole' is a prostrate form, slow growing and hugging the ground very tightly, being very attractive if trailed over a large stone or rock.

Tsuga canadensis 'Pendula'

P. 30–50cm. x S. 75cm.–1m.
U.H. 2–3m. x U.S. 6–10m.
This, the most widely grown cultivar of the species, is also often listed as *T. c.* 'Sargentii'. 'Pendula' makes a low bush with overlapping drooping branchlets wider than high and eventually becoming quite large. Many specimens are seen which have been trained upwards to a required height with the branches cascading downwards. Likewise the plant is most effective on a large rock outcrop as can be seen from the specimen at the R.H.S. Gardens, Wisley, Surrey, England. For either purpose it is a most useful and attractive plant.

Tsuga heterophylla

L. 5–6m.   U.H. 50–60m.
The "Western Hemlock" makes a much larger tree than the Eastern Hemlock, but has the same graceful habit. It is again too large a tree to be considered for all but the most spacious gardens but makes a very beautiful specimen. It is grown extensively in North America for timber and is now used in Great Britain for that purpose. This species dislikes alkaline soils and will thrive best in deep loamy soils with adequate moisture.

Tsuga canadensis 'Pendula'. – *This plant is about 6 years old.*

FOLIAGE

A close look at some Species and Cultivars

1. *Abies nordmanniana.*
2. *Abies pinsapo.*
3. *Cedrus atlantica. Foliage and cones.*
4. *Chamaecyparis lawsoniana* 'Allumii'.

1

3

2

4

5. *Chamaecyparis lawsoniana* 'Stewartii'.
6. *Juniperus x media* 'Pfitzeriana Aurea'.
7. *Juniperus sabina.*
8. *Juniperus chinensis* 'Pyramidalis'.

5

7

6

8

FOLIAGE

(continued)

9. *Calocedrus decurrens.*
10. *Pinus mugo.*

11. *Picea pungens.*
12. *Picea orientalis.*

9

11

10

12

13. *Taxus baccata.*

14. *Thuja occidentalis.*

15. *Below.* A most attractive selection of cones which are an added attraction on many conifers.

1. *Pinus pinaster*
2. *Pseudotsuga menziesii*
3. *Pinus monticola*
4. *Pinus heldreichii*
   leucodermis
5. *Picea abies*

6. *Pinus sylvestris*
7. *Cupressus sempervirens*
8. *Picea abies*
   (chewed by squirrel !)
9. *Pinus sylvestris*
10. *Pinus radiata*

11. *Pinus strobus*
12. *Cedrus atlantica*
13. *Pinus griffithii*
   (P. wallichiana)
14. *Pinus contorta*
15. *Pinus nigra maritima*

15.

*Two colourful views of conifers and heathers
in the garden at Foxhollow Windlesham, Surrey.*

INDEX

Synonyms see page 22

PAGE

ABIES 24
— *balsamea* 'Hudsonia' 24
— *concolor* 25
— *concolor* 'Compacta' 24
— *delavayi var. forestii* 26
— *grandis* 26
— *koreana* 27
— *lasiocarpa* 27
— *lasiocarpa* 'Compacta' 27
— *nordmanniana* 27
— *pinsapo* 28
— *pinsapo* 'Glauca' 28
— *procera* 28

ARAUCARIA 29
— *araucana* 29

CALOCEDRUS = LIBOCEDRUS 30
— *decurrens* 30
— *decurrens* 'Aureovariegata' 30

CEDRUS 31
— *atlantica* 'Aurea' 31
— *atlantica* 'Glauca' 31
— *atlantica* 'Glauca Pendula' 32
— *brevifolia* 35
— *deodara* 35
— *deodara* 'Aurea' 35
— *libani* 36
— *libani* 'Nana' 36
— *libani* 'Sargentii' 36

CEPHALOTAXUS 37
— *harringtonia var. drupacea.* 37

CHAMAECYPARIS 38
— *lawsoniana* 38
— *lawsoniana* 'Albovariegata' 38
— *lawsoniana* 'Alumii' 38
— *lawsoniana* 'Columnaris' 39
— *lawsoniana* 'Ellwoodii' 40
— *lawsoniana* 'Erecta Viridis' 41
— *lawsoniana* 'Fletcheri' 42
— *lawsoniana* 'Forsteckensis' 43
— *lawsoniana* 'Gimbornii' 43
— *lawsoniana* 'Green Pillar' 43
— *lawsoniana* 'Intertexta' 44
— *lawsoniana* 'Kilmacurragh' 44
— *lawsoniana* 'Knowfieldensis'. 44
— *lawsoniana* 'Lane' 44
— *lawsoniana* 'Lutea' 45
— *lawsoniana* 'Maas' 46
— *lawsoniana* 'Minima Aurea' 46
— *lawsoniana* 'Minima Glauca'. 47
— *lawsoniana* 'Nana Albospica'. 47
— *lawsoniana* 'Pembury Blue' 48
— *lawsoniana* 'Pottenii' 48
— *lawsoniana* 'Pygmaea Argentea' 49
— *lawsoniana* 'Spek' 49
— *lawsoniana* 'Stewartii' 49
— *lawsoniana* 'Tamariscifolia' 51
— *lawsoniana* 'Triomf van. Boskoop' 51
— *lawsoniana* 'Westermannii' 52
— *lawsoniana* 'W. Churchill' 52
— *lawsoniana* 'Wissellii' 52
— *nootkatensis* 54
— *nootkatensis* 'Compacta' 54
— *nootkatensis* 'Glauca' 54
— *nootkatensis* 'Lutea' 55
— *nootkatensis* 'Pendula' 55
— *obtusa* 55
— *obtusa* 'Crippsii' 57
— *obtusa* 'Intermedia' 57
— *obtusa* 'Kosteri' 57
— *obtusa* 'Nana' 58
— *obtusa* 'Nana Aurea' 58
— *obtusa* 'Nana Gracilis' 58
— *obtusa* 'Nana Lutea' 59
— *obtusa* 'Pygmaea' 59
— *obtusa* 'Tetragona Aurea' 59
— *pisifera* 61
— *pisifera* 'Boulevard' 61
— *pisifera* 'Filifera Aurea' 61
— *pisifera* 'Nana' 61
— *pisifera* 'Plumosa Aurea' 62
— *pisifera* 'Plumosa Aurea Nana' 62
— *pisifera* 'Plumosa Rogersii' 62
— *pisifera* 'Squarrosa Sulphurea' 62
— *thyoides* 63
— *thyoides* 'Andelyensis' 63
— *thyoides* 'Ericoides' 63

PAGE

CRYPTOMERIA 65
— *japonica* 'Elegans' 65
— *japonica* 'Globosa Nana'. 65
— *japonica* 'Lobbii Nana' 65
— *japonica* 'Spiralis' 66
— *japonica* 'Vilmoriniana' 66

CUPRESSUS 69
— *glabra* 69
— *macrocarpa* 69
— *macrocarpa* 'Goldcrest' 70
— *sempervirens* 'Stricta' 70

x CUPRESSOCYPARIS *leylandii* 70

GINGKO 72

JUNIPERUS 73
— *chinensis* 'Aurea' 74
— *chinensis* 'Japonica' 74
— *chinensis* 'Kaizuka' 75
— *chinensis* 'Pyramidalis' 75
— *communis* 76
— *communis* 'Compressa' 76
— *communis* 'Depressa Aurea' 76
— *communis* 'Hibernica' 77
— *communis* 'Repanda' 77
— *conferta* 78
— *davurica* 'Expansa Aureospicata' 79
— *horizontalis* 79
— *horizontalis* 'Bar Harbor' 79
— *horizontalis* 'Douglasii' 80
— *horizontalis* 'Glauca' 80
— *horizontalis* 'Montana' 81
— *horizontalis* 'Plumosa' 81
— *horizontalis* 'Wiltonii' 81
— *X media* 82
— *X media* 'Blaauw' 82
— *X media* 'Hetzii' 82
— *X media* 'Old Gold' 82
— *X media* 'Pfitzeriana' 82
— *X media* 'Pfitzeriana Aurea'. 84
— *X media* 'Plumosa Aurea' 85
— *procumbens* 85
— *procumbens* 'Nana' 85
— *recurva* 'Embley Park' 85
— *sabina* 86
— *sabina* 'Arcadia' 86
— *sabina* 'Blue Danube' 86
— *sabina* 'Tamariscifolia' 86
— *sargentii* 87
— *scopulorum* 87
— *scopulorum* 'Blue Heaven'. 87
— *scopulorum* 'Gray Gleam' 87
— *scopulorum* 'Skyrocket' 88
— *scopulorum* 'Springbank' 89
— *scopulorum* 'Table Top Blue' 89
— *squamata* 90
— *squamata* 'Blue Star' 90
— *squamata* 'Meyeri' 90
— *virginiana* 90
— *virginiana* 'Burkii' 91
— *virginiana* 'Grey Owl' 91

LARIX 92
— *decidua* 92
— *kaempferi* 92

METASEQUOIA 94
— *glyptostroboides* 94

PICEA 95
— *abies* 95
— *abies* 'Acrocona' 95
— *abies* 'Clanbrassiliana' 96
— *abies* 'Gregoryana' 96
— *abies* 'Nidiformis' 96
— *abies* 'Ohlendorffii' 96
— *abies* 'Procumbens' 97
— *abies* 'Pumila' 97
— *abies* 'Reflexa' 97
— *breweriana* 99
— *engelmannii* 99
— *glauca* 'Albertiana Conica' 99
— *mariana* 'Nana' 99
— *omorika* 100
— *omorika* 'Pendula' 101
— *orientalis* 101
— *orientalis* 'Aurea' 101
— *pungens* 102
— *pungens* 'Endtz' 102
— *pungens glauca* 102

PAGE

PICEA *pungens* 'Globosa' 102
— *pungens* 'Koster' 103
— *pungens* 'Prostrata' 103
— *pungens* 'Moerheimii' 104
— *pungens* 'Montgomery' 104

PINUS 106
— *aristata* 107
— *ayacahuite* 107
— *cembra* 109
— *contorta* 109
— *densiflora* 109
— *densiflora* 'Umbraculifera' 109
— *griffithii* 109
— *heldreichii* 'Compact Gem' 110
— *mugo* 110
— *mugo* 'Gnom' 110
— *mugo var. pumilio* 110
— *nigra* 112
— *nigra* 'Hornibrookiana' 113
— *nigra var. maritima* 113
— *nigra* 'Pygmaea' 113
— *parviflora* 114
— *parviflora* 'Glauca' 114
— *pinea* 115
— *ponderosa* 115
— *pumila* 116
— *strobus* 116
— *strobus* 'Nana' 116
— *sylvestris* 117
— *sylvestris* 'Aurea' 118
— *sylvestris* 'Beuvronensis' 118
— *sylvestris* 'Watereri' 119

PODOCARPUS 120
— *nivalis* 120

PSEUDOTSUGA 121
— *menziesii* 121
— *menziesii* 'Fletcheri' 121

SCIADOPITYS 122
— *verticillata* 122

SEQUOIA 123
— *sempervirens* 123
— *sempervirens* 'Adpressa' 123

SEQUOIADENDRON 124
— *giganteum* 124

TAXODIUM 125
— *distichum* 125

TAXUS 126
— *baccata* 126
— *baccata* 'Adpressa Variegata' 126
— *baccata* 'Dovastonii Aurea' 126
— *baccata* 'Elegantissima' 126
— *baccata* 'Fastigiata Aurea' 129
— *baccata* 'Repandens' 129
— *baccata* 'Semperaurea' 130
— *cuspidata* 130
— *X media* 131

THUJA 132
— *occidentalis* 132
— *occidentalis* 'Hetz Midget' 132
— *occidentalis* 'Holmstrup' 133
— *occidentalis* 'Lutea Nana' 133
— *occidentalis* 'Wareana Lutescens' 133
— *occidentalis* 'Pyramidalis' 134
— *occidentalis* 'Recurva Nana' 134
— *occidentalis* 'Rheingold' 134
— *occidentalis* 'Smaragd' 135
— *occidentalis* 'Woodwardii' 135
— *orientalis* 135
— *orientalis* 'Aurea Nana' 137
— *orientalis* 'Conspicua' 137
— *orientalis* 'Elegantissima' 137
— *orientalis* 'Juniperoides' 137
— *orientalis* 'Rosedalis' 137
— *plicata* 138
— *plicata* 'Atrovirens' 138
— *plicata* 'Rogersii' 138
— *plicata* 'Stoneham Gold' 139
— *plicata* 'Zebrina' 139

THUJOPSIS 140
— *dolobrata* 140

TSUGA 140
— *canadensis* 141
— *canadensis* 'Bennett' 140
— *canadensis* 'Pendula' 141
— *heterophylla* 141

FOLIAGE .... 142 to 145

© Éditions Floraisse - All rights reserved - May 1981 - Legally deposed N° 17 - 4e Édition